COOK THE
WEEK IN
2 HOURS

Batch cook a whole week's meals
to save time and money

CAROLINE PESSIN

photography by Charly Deslandes

hamlyn

COOK THE WEEK IN 2 HOURS

Batch cook a whole week's meals & save time and money

Preface

If, like me, you are a fan of all foods homemade and seasonal, but at the same time your workdays are so full you have neither the time nor the energy during the week to cook…

If, like me, you try to offer your family healthy and balanced meals that appeal to both adults and kids…

If, like me, you find that ordering takeout or delivery leaves a large hole in your food budget…

And, if the question 'What's for dinner?' each night from your family has become your weekly obsession…then you will love the cooking method in this book, a method often referred to as 'batch cooking' or 'the meal-prep method', consisting of preparing meals in advance for every night of the week.

Since I discovered this method, I save money and eat a balanced diet, and at the same time free up my weeknights to enjoy more time with my family and reduce the stress caused from having to plan and prepare a meal each night.

On weekends, this method takes about two hours of my time to prep, marinate and cook several dishes at once. Then, during the week, I simply reheat, assemble or finish the meal with some quick final steps, and dinner is ready!

Several of my friends have tried this approach and they love it. And I'm convinced once you try it, you'll love it, too.

Introduction

What a joy it is to come home each night from work without the worry of deciding what to make for dinner. Nothing offers more peace of mind during the week than knowing you will have to spend very little time cooking at the end of the day, and that you will be able to enjoy a delicious and balanced meal that requires minimal clearing up.

The following questions each night are familiar to many of us: 'What am I going to make for dinner?' 'Do I have what I need in the fridge?' 'How will I be able to cook a delicious and healthy meal and spend time with the kids, give them their baths, help them with homework, etc.?'

When we feel overwhelmed with the answers to these questions, we often end up giving in to what's easiest: just boiling some pasta, or heating a frozen readymeal or opting for a delivery or takeaway – all of which are less healthy and less economical choices.

But by adopting a different approach to organizing your meals and cooking, it is possible to alleviate the stress of making dinner each night for your family.

The idea is simple: during the weekend set aside about two hours for cooking an entire week's worth of meals.

In this book, we have laid out for you sixteen varied and balanced menus, grouped by the seasons. The menus are designed to feed a family of four, with enough in quantity to feed two adults and two teenagers. If you have small children, or if you are only three people, the leftovers make a great lunch.

Each menu has seven recipes: five main courses and two starters (for evenings when the main courses are lighter). We chose not to include desserts because most of us simply eat a piece of fruit or perhaps some ice cream after dinner; and many of us like to leave our sweeter indulgences for the weekends.

With this method, you no longer have to worry about what to make for dinner Monday to Friday or have to do last-minute shopping, and you will spend fifteen minutes or less in the kitchen each night – that's a promise!

To use this method of cooking, simply follow these steps:

1. Choose one of the seasonal menus that appeals to you.

2. Do your food shopping in advance of when you want to cook. Each menu's ingredients can be found easily in most supermarkets. Only in a very few cases will it be necessary to make a quick trip to a speciality food store or market.

3. Choose a day when you have a free block of two hours in front of you. If you are cooking at the weekend, it is best to cook on Sunday rather than Saturday, to ensure everything stays its freshest throughout the week and to cut down on the number of meals you have to freeze.

4. Before you begin cooking, set out all the listed ingredients on your kitchen work surface. This is a tip for saving even more time because it avoids trips to the refrigerator or store cupboard each time you need something.

5. Before you begin cooking, set out all of the necessary utensils and equipment that are listed. If you do this, you will have everything at your fingertips while you cook.

6. Follow the steps of the recipes as they are written, as they were developed according to actual preparation times.

7. Store the finished dishes and ingredients as instructed at the end of each cooking session. In general, dishes to be served Monday to Wednesday can be refrigerated, while those to be served Thursday and Friday should be frozen (although there are a few menus where nothing needs to be frozen).

The result? During each night of the week, all you have to do is follow the instructions for assembling, reheating or completing the meals with some quick, final steps. In total, you will spend fifteen minutes or less in your kitchen each night. Some nights, there is nothing to do except reheat a dish. Other nights you'll need to do some last-minute cooking, some quick final prep or just combine some ingredients.

What are the advantages of this method?

Firstly, this method offers undeniable peace of mind during the week by eliminating the hassle of deciding what to prepare for dinner as well as eliminating the need to do last-minute shopping at the end of the day.

Secondly, this method is a real time-saver because not only will you spend much less time cooking, you will also spend less time washing up and putting away the dishes. You can use the extra time you gain each night by relaxing or spending time with your family.

Thirdly, this method offers a variety of balanced meals with delicious homemade flavours without all the additives and preservatives you find in some commercially produced or restaurant-prepared meals.

And finally, this method offers considerable savings for your food budget because there are fewer pricey takeaway meals as well as less waste, as we have created these menus to use up each ingredient entirely by the end of the week – it's a 'zero waste' kitchen!

What are the disadvantages of this method?

Spending two hours cooking on a single day can be a bit tiring. You may feel you are wasting part of your time off, which often already seems too short. But you will see that the relaxation provided by this method during the week makes these two hours well worth it. In addition, we have done everything to make the cooking sessions easy: step-by-step preparation is provided and the photos allow you to see what the finished dishes should look like.

What equipment do I need?

You will need an oven with at least two shelves and a hob with at least three burners. During the cooking session, all the cooking is done simultaneously, which again saves time as well as energy costs for running the stove and oven.

For the equipment and containers needed for preparing the menus, *see* page 12.

Before you start:

* Make room in your freezer. Maybe plan some 'empty-the-freezer' meals beforehand to free up freezer space.

* Before leaving for the supermarket, sort through your refrigerator, discard any stale or questionable foods, clean the shelves with white vinegar to remove odours and bacteria and consume any leftovers you find.

We challenge you to test this method with at least one menu and see the positive change it has on your weeknights. You may not stop after just one menu but quickly adopt this method for every week!

Refrigeration

Expected shelf life:

1 week:
* Washed lettuce
* Washed herbs
* Cut vegetables
* Chopped onions and garlic
* Vinaigrette

5 days:
* Hard-boiled eggs
* Hummus
* Home-cooked pulses (lentils, chickpeas, dried beans, etc.)

3 to **4** days:
* Cooked grains (rice, bulgur)
* Cooked vegetables
* Stock- and cream-based soups, velouté
* Meatless gratins

2 days:
* Marinated meats
* Cooked fish and meats
* Quiches, flaky pastries

Tips:
* Do not prepare potatoes until the last minute: when sliced and kept raw they will oxidize, and when cooked in advance they will take on a bad flavour.
* For grains that cook quickly (rice, pasta, couscous), be sure to cook them at the last minute for the best flavour and optimal texture.
* Store stewed dishes and soups in the pans or pots in which they were prepared so that you can easily reheat them.
* Frozen homemade dishes should be consumed within two months for the best texture.

Essential equipment

For cooking:

For the menus in this book, make sure you have the following cookware to hand:
* 1 lidded cast-iron casserole or stockpot (even better if you have both)
* 1 sauté pan
* 1 frying pan
* 3 saucepans of different sizes
* Optional: 1 wok, 1 steam cooker

The equipment needed for these menus is very basic, requiring no professional-level equipment at all: mixing bowls, ramekins, colander, sieve, baking tray, gratin dish or shallow baking dish, flan tin, round cake tin, loaf tin, salad spinner, stick blender, food mill (or potato masher), small food processor, zester or grater and a skimmer or slotted spoon.

For storing:

This book requires foods and prepared dishes to be stored. It is essential, therefore, that you have several airtight containers to hand. Choose glass containers, which are more hygienic than plastic and can be placed safely in the oven or microwave. You will find many of these types of containers at IKEA or online at reasonable prices.

You will need a maximum of:
* 1 very large container for storing salads
* 3 large containers
* 5 medium containers
* 3 small containers
* 2 small airtight containers for storing chopped onions and garlic, to seal off odours
* 1 (1.5-litre) glass jar for storing soups and gazpachos

Also, be sure to keep in your store cupboard: cling film, freezer and airtight storage bags, kitchen paper, baking paper.

Basic stores

The following ingredients are used frequently in the menus, so be sure to keep these stocked:

* Basic herbs and spices: bay leaves, dried thyme, herbes de Provence, ground cinnamon, curry powder, ground cumin, ras el hanout, whole nutmeg
* Table salt, sea salt flakes
* Black pepper
* Sunflower oil
* Olive oil
* Tomato ketchup
* Plain flour
* Baking powder
* Cornflour
* Honey
* Mustard
* Passata
* Quinoa
* White rice
* Brown rice
* Couscous
* Dried pasta
* Quick-cook grains (such as durum wheat, bulgur, etc.)
* Dried breadcrumbs
* Lentils
* Soy sauce
* Balsamic vinegar
* Wine vinegar

Spring

Menu #1

Menu #1

Shopping list

Menu #1

Fruit / Vegetables

* 1 bunch of carrots
* 12 green asparagus spears
* 8 small turnips
* 4 stems of cherry tomatoes (on the vine)
* 1.5kg Charlotte (waxy) potatoes
* 1 small lemon
* 1 bunch of spring onions
* 1 bunch of parsley
* 1 bunch of basil
* 6 garlic cloves

Basics

* Plain flour
* Olive oil
* Salt, black pepper

Meat / Fish

* 1kg leg of lamb
* 800g fresh cod loin strips

Refrigerator

* 115g grated Parmesan cheese
* 330ml double cream
* 50g unsalted butter

Store cupboard

* 500g drained canned cannellini beans, liquid reserved
* 400g short pasta
* 50g pine nuts
* Tahini (optional)
* Ground cumin
* Dried breadcrumbs

Monday

Garlic leg of lamb, roasted vegetables, cannellini beans

Tuesday

Starter
Asparagus soup

Main
Herb-crusted fresh cod

Wednesday

Shepherd's pie

Thursday

Starter
White-bean hummus, vegetable sticks

Main
Pasta with asparagus and fresh cod

Friday

Minestrone

Steps

Set up

If you have enough work space, set out all the ingredients needed for this cooking session. This includes everything except 3 stems of the cherry tomatoes, the pasta and the breadcrumbs.

This allows you to have everything at your fingertips and to not lose time searching for the ingredients in the store cupboard or refrigerator.

Set out the necessary equipment:

* 2 baking dishes (1 large for the leg of lamb)
* 1 gratin dish (or shallow baking dish)
* 1 food mill (or potato masher)
* 1 sauté pan
* 1 large saucepan
* 1 medium saucepan
* 1 stick blender
* 1 food processor
* 3 containers: 2 medium + 1 large
* Clingfilm

Everything is now ready for a cooking time of 1¾ hours.

1 Preheat the oven to 180°C/gas mark 4. Peel the garlic cloves, cut them in half lengthways, and remove any green sprout from the centres. Place the leg of lamb in the large baking dish. Make 6 deep incisions in the lamb using a knife. Insert a garlic clove half into each incision. Place the remaining 6 garlic halves in a small dish and set aside. Season the lamb with salt and pepper, then rub it all over with pieces of the butter. Bake for 40 minutes.

2 Bring 2 saucepans of salted water to a boil: one large and one medium. Peel the potatoes, turnips and asparagus. Cut the potatoes in half crossways and place them in the large saucepan of boiling water.

Cook for 20 minutes. Cut 2 of the turnips into quarters. Cut 2 of the turnips into sticks. Leave the 4 remaining turnips whole. Place the turnip quarters and the asparagus in the medium saucepan of boiling water and cook for 10 minutes.

3 Cut off and discard the root ends of the spring onions and strip off the first layer of skin. Chop the onions, and add half of them to the saucepan with the turnips and asparagus. Add 1 garlic clove half to the pan.

4 Peel the carrots. Leave 6 of the carrots whole. Cut half of the remaining carrots into rounds and the other half into sticks. Place the carrot sticks in a medium container. Add the turnip sticks to the container; the raw vegetable sticks will be used for dipping in the hummus.

5 Remove 6 asparagus spears from the saucepan. Rinse them under cold water to maintain their colour, then cut them into pieces. Set them aside in the empty medium container.

6 Drain the water from the saucepan containing the remaining asparagus. Add half the cream, ½ teaspoon of salt, a little pepper and 2 of the cooked potatoes. Blend using the stick blender until smooth.

7 When the lamb has cooked for 40 minutes, add the 4 whole turnips, the whole carrots, 1 stem of the cherry tomatoes on the vine, and 200g of the beans with their liquid to the baking dish. Season with salt and pepper, and cook for 20 minutes more, or until the lamb is cooked to your liking.

8 Wash and pat dry the parsley and basil.

9 Prepare the herb crust for the cod. In the food processor, place 30g of the pine nuts, 30g of flour, half the parsley, half the basil, a garlic clove half and a little salt and pepper. Process to form a paste. Spread the paste over the top of the cod strips. Place the cod in the gratin dish, and bake for 15 minutes, or until cooked through.

10 In the sauté pan, heat 1 tablespoon of olive oil until warm. Add the remaining chopped spring onions, carrot rounds, and ½ teaspoon of salt. Cook for 5 minutes, or until softened. Add 500ml of water, and cook for 10 minutes more.

11 Meanwhile, make the pesto. In the food processor used to make the herb crust (there is no need to wash it), place the remaining pine nuts, 2 garlic clove halves, the remaining basil, half the Parmesan, ½ teaspoon of salt, and 1 pinch of pepper. Pulse to combine while slowly adding 1 tablespoon of olive oil.

12 Dice 2 of the cooked potatoes, and add them to the sauté pan with the spring onions and carrots along with 150g of the beans. Turn off the heat, and add the pesto. Stir to combine, then transfer the minestrone to the large container.

It's all done! Leave to cool.

Place in the refrigerator:
* The lamb and the accompanying vegetables, directly in the baking dish, covered with clingfilm (keeps for 2 days)
* The asparagus soup, in the saucepan (keeps for 3 days)
* The herb-crusted cod, if you are serving it within 2 days of preparing it
* The white-bean hummus, covered with clingfilm (keeps for 5 days)
* The vegetable sticks (keeps for 1 week)

Place in the freezer:
* The herb-crusted cod, if you are serving it more than 2 days after preparing it
* The Shepherd's pie, in its serving dish, covered with clingfilm
* The container with the asparagus pieces and cod
* The minestrone

13 Mash the remaining potatoes using the food mill (or potato masher) then combine them with the remaining cream, ½ teaspoon of salt and a pinch of pepper.

14 Bone the leg of lamb and cut it into 6 slices. In the food processor or using the stick blender, process the 2 least attractive pieces together with 2 tablespoons of parsley leaves, 2 cooked carrots and a little of the cooking juices. Place the mixture in the empty baking dish, and cover it with the mashed potatoes. Clean the food processor. Return the remaining lamb pieces to the large baking dish.

15 Make the white-bean hummus. Place the remaining beans (drained), the remaining garlic halves, 1 teaspoon of tahini (if using), the juice of the lemon and 1 pinch of cumin in the food processor. Process until smooth. Transfer the mixture to an attractive serving bowl. Chop the remaining parsley. Sprinkle half the parsley on top. Sprinkle the remaining parsley on top of the leg of lamb.

16 Flake a quarter of the cooked herb-crusted cod. Add the flaked cod to the container with the asparagus.

Menu #1

Menu #1

Monday

Garlic leg of lamb, roasted vegetables, cannellini beans

Reheating time:
10 minutes

Ingredients: the baking dish with the lamb and vegetables
Preheat the oven to 180°C/gas mark 4. Reheat the leg of lamb and the accompanying vegetables for 10 minutes. Serve!
For Tuesday, if you have frozen the herb-crusted cod, remove it from the freezer and defrost it in the refrigerator.

Cooking and reheating time:
10 minutes

Tuesday

Starter
Asparagus soup

Main
Herb-crusted fresh cod

Ingredients: the asparagus soup, herb-crusted cod, 2 stems of cherry tomatoes, olive oil
Preheat the oven to 200°C/gas mark 6. In a saucepan, reheat the soup for 10 minutes. Roast the cherry tomatoes for 7 minutes with a drizzle of olive oil.
Lower the temperature of the oven to 150°C/gas mark 2. Add the cod and reheat for 3 minutes.
For Wednesday, remove the Shepherd's pie from the freezer and defrost it in the refrigerator.

Wednesday

Shepherd's pie

Reheating time:
10 minutes

Ingredients: the Shepherd's pie, some dried breadcrumbs
Preheat the oven to 220°C/gas mark 7. Sprinkle the top of the Shepherd's pie with breadcrumbs and bake for 10 minutes. Serve!
For Thursday, remove the container of asparagus and cod from the freezer and defrost it in the refrigerator.

Thursday

Starter
White-bean hummus, vegetable sticks

Main
Pasta with asparagus and fresh cod

<u>**Cooking and reheating time:**</u>
15 minutes
<u>**Preparation time:**</u>
1 minute

Ingredients: the raw vegetable sticks, hummus, pasta, the container with the asparagus pieces and cod, remaining Parmesan
Cook the pasta according to the packet instructions.
Set aside one-third of the pasta for Friday's minestrone in a container in the refrigerator. Reheat the asparagus and the cod in the microwave. Add them to the remaining pasta, and stir briefly to combine. Sprinkle with the Parmesan.
<u>**For Friday, remove the minestrone from the freezer and defrost it in the refrigerator.**</u>

<u>**Reheating time:**</u>
10 minutes

Friday

Minestrone

Ingredients: the remaining cooked pasta, the minestrone, remaining cherry tomatoes
Reheat the minestrone in a large saucepan with the cherry tomatoes for 10 minutes. Add the cooked pasta, and serve.

Menu #2

Shopping basket

Menu #2

Fruit / Vegetables

* 2 bunches of watercress
* 1 large bag (about 250 g) baby spinach (sell-by date > 4 days)
* 1 bunch of radishes
* 1 bunch of spring onions
* 3 heads of romaine lettuce
* 1 large potato
* 1 organic lime
* 1 lemon
* 1 bunch fresh coriander
* 1 bunch of tarragon
* 3 shallots
* 8 garlic cloves
* 1 (5cm) knob of fresh root ginger

Meat / Fish

* 1 (200g) salmon fillet
* 1 monkfish tail (ask your fishmonger to skin the fish and cut the tail into cubes)
* 8 small boneless, skinless chicken breasts

Refrigerator

* 4 large eggs
* 1 small wedge of Parmesan cheese
* 250g mascarpone cheese
* 250g ricotta cheese
* 450ml crème fraîche or natural yogurt
* 330ml double cream
* 2 sheets of ready-rolled shortcrust pastry

Basics

* Just over 200ml passata
* Mustard
* Sunflower oil
* Olive oil
* Salt, black pepper

Store cupboard

* 1 large loaf wholegrain bread
* 400ml coconut milk
* ⅔ teaspoon green curry paste
* 2 cardamom pods
* 1 tablespoon tandoori spice blend
* 200g red lentils
* 500g white rice
* 8 anchovies
* Worcestershire sauce
* Tabasco sauce

Monday

Salmon and
watercress pie

Tuesday

Starter
Radish toasts

Main
Tarragon chicken

Wednesday

Lentil dhal

Thursday

Starter
Creamy radish-leaf
spread

Main
Caesar salad

Friday

Green curry monkfish

Set up

If you have enough work space, set out all the ingredients needed for this cooking session. This includes everything except the baby spinach, lettuce, lemon, 1 garlic clove, cream, chicken breasts, Parmesan, rice, Worcestershire sauce, Tabasco sauce, and anchovies. This allows you to have everything at your fingertips and to not lose time searching for the ingredients in the store cupboard or refrigerator.

Set out the necessary equipment:

* 1 food processor
* 1 salad spinner (or large bowl and clean tea towel)
* 1 frying pan
* 1 (20cm) round cake tin
* 1 sauté pan
* 1 stick blender
* 1 small saucepan
* 1 large saucepan
* 1 small grater (for the lime zest and fresh ginger)
* 1 small bowl
* 1 (1.5-litre) glass jar (for storing the radish-greens spread)
* 7 containers: 2 large + 1 medium + 4 small
* 1 airtight storage bag, kitchen paper, clingfilm

Everything is now ready for a cooking time of 2 hours.

1 Cut off and discard the stems from the watercress. Wash and dry the leaves using the salad spinner (or fill a large bowl with water and wash the leaves, then gently pat them dry with the tea towel), then roughly chop them. Set aside 1 handful of the chopped leaves in a bowl.

2 Peel and chop the shallots and 7 of the garlic cloves.

3 In the frying pan, heat 1 tablespoon of olive oil until warm. Add one-third of the shallots, ½ teaspoon of the chopped garlic and ½ teaspoon of salt. Cook for 2 minutes, or until softened. Add the chopped watercress leaves (except what was set aside in the

bowl), and cook for 5 more minutes over high heat, or until the liquid has evaporated.

4 Meanwhile, fill the small saucepan with water, bring it to a boil, and cook 1 egg for 10 minutes.

5 Break the remaining 3 eggs into a bowl. Set aside half a raw egg yolk (it will be used to brush the pastry). In the food processor, place the raw eggs, mascarpone, ½ teaspoon of salt and a little pepper. Pulse to combine. Add the cooked watercress mixture and pulse again to combine.

6 Preheat the oven to 180°C/gas mark 4. Cut the salmon into small cubes and add them to the food processor. Grease the cake tin and line it with one of the pastry sheets. Fold and gently press any excess pastry down onto the interior sides of the tin.

Cut out a circle from the second pastry sheet the same diameter as the tin. Scrape the watercress-salmon mixture into the pastry-lined cake tin, then place the pastry circle on top. Tuck the excess pastry down into the tin along the edges, and brush the top with the reserved half egg yolk. Using a knife, cut a small hole in the centre of the pastry lid, then roll up a small piece of baking paper and stick it into the hole to create a little 'chimney'. Bake for 50 minutes, or until golden and flaky on top.

7 Cut off the radish leaves level with the tops of the radishes. Place the leaves in the salad spinner and gently wash them several times (or in a large bowl with fresh water). Wash the radishes, cut them into rounds, then place them in a small container.

8 In the large saucepan, heat 1 tablespoon of olive oil until warm. Add half the remaining chopped shallots, ½ teaspoon of chopped garlic and ½ teaspoon of salt. Cook for 5 minutes over very low heat until softened. Meanwhile, peel the potato and chop into small dice. Add the diced potato to the saucepan, then add 400ml of water. Cook for 10 minutes.

9 Rinse and finely chop the spring onions. Wash and gently dry the coriander and tarragon. Peel the ginger.

10 To the large saucepan with the potatoes, add the radish leaves, the reserved watercress, 1 sprig of tarragon, and 1 tablespoon of the chopped green portion of the onions. Cook for 3 minutes. Add 3 tablespoons of the ricotta cheese, then blend using the stick blender. Transfer the mixture to the glass jar, leaving a little room at the top.

11 In the food processor, place 2 tablespoons of chopped spring onions, 1 teaspoon of chopped garlic, one-third of the coriander with the stems, half the ginger and all of the green curry paste. Process until smooth.

12 Prepare the green curry monkfish. In the sauté pan, bring half the coconut milk to a boil and let it reduce by half. Stir in the green curry mixture, and boil for 1 minute. Add the monkfish cubes, and cook, uncovered, for 5 minutes over high heat. At the end of the cooking time, grate the lime zest into the pan, then add the juice of half the lemon. Transfer the mixture to the medium container. Rinse and wipe out the pan.

It's all done! Leave to cool.

Place in the refrigerator:
* The hard-boiled egg (keeps for 5 days)
* The salmon and watercress pie, in its tin (keeps for 2 days)
* The lentil dhal (keeps for 4 days)
* The remaining chopped spring onions (keeps for 1 week)
* The radish slices (keeps for 1 week)
* The tarragon sauce (keeps for 3 days)
* The remaining coriander and tarragon, in an airtight container between two sheets of kitchen paper (keeps for 1 week)
* The 8 slices of bread, in the airtight storage bag (keeps for 4 days)

Place in the freezer:
* The green curry monkfish
* The creamy radish-leaf spread

Store cupboard:
* The croutons

13 Prepare the lentil dhal. Grate the remaining ginger. In the sauté pan, heat 1 tablespoon of olive oil until warm. Add half the remaining chopped garlic and shallots, 1 teaspoon of salt, the tandoori spice blend, the cardamom pods and the grated ginger. Cook for 1 minute, then add the lentils, passata and 300ml of water. Simmer for 15 minutes over a low heat. If the dhal becomes too thick, add a little more water during the cooking time.

14 Slice 8 attractive slices of bread and set them aside. Cut the remaining bread (the two heels) into cubes. Place the bread cubes in a small bowl with 2 tablespoons of olive oil, ½ teaspoon of salt and half the remaining garlic. Stir to combine, then bake at 180°C/gas mark 4 for 10 minutes, or until the bread cubes are golden. Place the croutons in a small container.

15 Once the lentils are tender, add the remaining coconut milk and the juice of the lime. Stir to combine for 1 minute on the heat.

16 Prepare the tarragon sauce. In the small saucepan, heat 1 teaspoon of olive oil until warm. Add the remaining garlic and shallots, then add ½ teaspoon of salt, and cook for 3 minutes, or until slightly softened. Add 2 tablespoons of mustard, the crème fraîche and three-quarters of the tarragon. Bring to a boil, cook for 2 minutes, then remove the pan from the heat and blend using the stick blender.

Menu #2

Monday

Salmon and watercress pie

Reheating time:
10 minutes

Ingredients: the salmon and watercress pie
Preheat the oven to 180°C/gas mark 4. Reheat the pie for 10 minutes.

Cooking time:
15 minutes
Preparation time:
10 minutes

Tuesday

Starter
Radish toasts

Main
Tarragon chicken

Ingredients: the 8 slices of bread, remaining ricotta cheese, radish slices, chopped spring onions, olive oil, chicken breasts, the tarragon sauce, remaining tarragon, salt and pepper
Toast the slices of bread. Spread some of the ricotta cheese on top of each slice, then top with a few radish slices, green onions and salt and pepper. Set aside several of the radish slices for Thursday. Chop the tarragon.
In a large frying pan, heat 2 tablespoons of olive oil until warm, and cook the chicken breasts for 15 minutes, or until cooked through. Remove 4 of the chicken breasts, and refrigerate in an airtight container for Thursday's Caesar salad. In the pan, bring the tarragon sauce to the boil. Sprinkle with chopped tarragon, and serve over the chicken breasts.

Wednesday

Lentil dhal

Cooking and reheating time:
10 minutes

Ingredients: the rice, lentil dhal, bag of baby spinach, remaining coriander, salt and pepper
Rinse the rice and cook it according to the packet instructions. Reheat the lentil dhal in a saucepan over low heat for 5 minutes. Add the baby spinach, season with salt and pepper, and cook over high heat for 5 more minutes. Serve the lentil dhal with half the rice and half the coriander. Place the remaining rice and coriander in the refrigerator to serve with the monkfish on Friday.
For Thursday, remove the radish-leaf spread from the freezer and defrost it in the refrigerator.

Thursday

Starter
Creamy radish-leaf spread

Main
Caesar salad

Reheating time:
10 minutes
Preparation time:
15 minutes

Ingredients: the radish-leaf spread, remaining radish slices, the heads of romaine, remaining 4 chicken breasts, the croutons, hard-boiled egg, garlic clove, anchovies, wedge of Parmesan, lemon half, sunflower oil, double cream, Tabasco sauce, Worcestershire sauce

In a saucepan, reheat the radish-leaf spread over low heat for 10 minutes. Distribute the remaining radish slices on top. Make the Caesar dressing. In the bowl of a food processor, add the peeled hard-boiled egg, half the Parmesan, the garlic and anchovies. Process until smooth. Add the juice of the lemon half, and process for 2 minutes. Add 70 ml of olive oil, the cream and several drops of Tabasco sauce and Worcestershire sauce. Pulse briefly to combine.

Wash and dry the lettuce leaves. Dress the leaves with some of the Caesar dressing. Cut the chicken breasts into thin strips, and season them with salt and pepper.

In a large bowl, combine the romaine leaves, chicken and croutons. Using a vegetable peeler, shave off large shavings of the remaining Parmesan. Serve with the remaining dressing. **For Friday, remove the green curry monkfish from the freezer and defrost it in the refrigerator.**

Reheating time:
10 minutes

Friday

Green curry monkfish

Ingredients: the green curry monkfish, remaining coriander, the remaining rice, salt and pepper

Reheat the monkfish in a saucepan, and reheat the rice according to the method you prefer. Serve the green curry monkfish over the rice. Season with salt and pepper, and sprinkle with the coriander.

Menu #3

Menu #3

Menu #3

Fruit / Vegetables

* 1 fennel bulb
* 1 lemon
* 1 lime
* 1 head of red leaf lettuce
* 1 bunch of carrots
* 100g bean sprouts
* 1kg spinach leaves, or 500g frozen chopped spinach
* 3 tomatoes
* 2 small cucumbers
* 400g broad beans in their pods, or 200g shelled and frozen
* 1 bunch spring onions
* 1 bunch of fresh coriander
* 1 (5cm) knob of fresh root ginger
* 4 garlic cloves

Meat / Fish

* 4 strips of skirt steak
* 4 thin turkey steaks
* 2 thin slices ham* (or turkey)
* 20 frozen raw, peeled prawns

Refrigerator

* 10 large eggs
* 250g ricotta cheese
* 115g grated Parmesan cheese
* 1 ball 225g fresh mozzarella cheese
* 330ml single cream
* 120–180g goats' cheese (coated with ash)

Basics

* Dried breadcrumbs
* Plain flour
* Mustard
* Dried thyme
* Vinegar
* Olive oil and sunflower oil
* Salt, black pepper

Store cupboard

* 2 cans albacore tuna (about 320g total)
* 8 anchovies
* 50g niçoise olives
* 200g pasta shells
* 250g quick-cook grains – such as durum wheat (Ebly brand), bulgur or mixed grains
* 200g rice noodles
* 200ml passata
* 1 baguette (purchased Thursday)
* Soy sauce
* Fish sauce

Monday

Starter
Fennel marinated in olive oil and lemon

Main
Turkey cordon bleu*

Tuesday

Marinated skirt steak, puréed baby carrots

Wednesday

Spinach and ricotta stuffed shells

Thursday

Salad Niçoise

Friday

Starter
Goats' cheese toasts

Main
Prawn pad thai

*For a menu without pork, replace the ham with slices of turkey breast.

Steps

Menu #3

Set up

If you have enough work space, set out all the ingredients needed for this cooking session. This includes everything except the lime, bean sprouts, prawns, 3 eggs, Parmesan, goats' cheese, tuna, anchovies, olives, grains, rice noodles and fish sauce. This allows you to have everything at your fingertips and to not lose time searching for the ingredients in the store cupboard or refrigerator. Set out the necessary equipment:

* 1 grater (for grating the carrots and ginger)
* 1 large baking dish
* 1 salad spinner (or large bowl and clean tea towel)
* 1 mixing bowl
* 1 sauté pan
* 1 small saucepan
* 1 medium saucepan
* 1 large saucepan
* 1 stick blender
* 1 skimmer (or slotted spoon)
* 1 food processor (or mandoline slicer or knife)
* 3 shallow bowls
* 10 containers: 3 large + 3 medium + 4 small
* 1 freezer bag (if you will be freezing the baguette), clingfilm, kitchen paper

Everything is now ready for a cooking time of 2 hours 10 minutes.

1 Rinse each leaf of the red lettuce under cold water. Gently dry the leaves in the salad spinner (or pat them dry with the tea towel), then place them in a large airtight container between 2 sheets of kitchen paper; the leaves will keep for up to 1 week in the refrigerator.

2 Remove any rubber bands from around the bunch of coriander, and immerse the coriander in cold water to wash it. Gently dry the coriander in the salad spinner (or pat dry with the towel), set aside 6 sprigs, and place the remaining sprigs in an airtight container between two sheets of kitchen paper for up to 1 week.

3 Wash the fresh spinach leaves, spin the leaves dry in the salad spinner (or gently pat dry with the towel), and roughly chop them. Peel and chop the garlic cloves.

4 In the sauté pan, heat 2 tablespoons of olive oil until warm. Add ½ teaspoon of chopped garlic, ½ teaspoon of salt and the chopped spinach, a little at a time. Cook for 15 minutes, uncovered, just until the water released by the spinach has evaporated.

5 Fill the large saucepan with salted water and bring it to a boil. Cook the pasta shells to al dente (still firm to the bite). Drain.

6 Add the cooked spinach to the mixing bowl. Add the ricotta, season with salt and pepper, and process with the stick blender until roughly blended.

7 Pour the passata into the large baking dish, and season with salt and pepper. Stuff the pasta shells with the ricotta-spinach mixture using a small spoon. Arrange the shells close together in the baking dish.

8 Fill the medium saucepan with salted water and bring it to a boil. Peel all of the carrots. Grate 2 of the carrots and place them in an airtight container. Cut the remaining carrots into rounds, and cook them for 20 minutes in the boiling water.

9 Fill the small saucepan with salted water and bring it to a boil. Shell the beans, and cook them for 2 minutes in the boiling water. Using the skimmer, remove the beans from the saucepan and rinse them under cold water. In the same saucepan of boiling water, boil 4 of the eggs for 10 minutes.

Menu #3

10 Very thinly slice the fennel bulb (using the mandoline, food processor or knife). Place the slices in a small container and sprinkle them with the juice from the lemon, 3 tablespoons of olive oil, ½ teaspoon of salt and a little pepper. Stir briefly to combine, and place them in the refrigerator to marinate.

11 Peel the ginger and cut into thirds. Drain the cooked carrots and return them to the saucepan. Using the stick blender, purée the cooked carrots with the cream, ½ teaspoon of salt, a little pepper and one-third of the ginger, and blend until smooth. Transfer to a container.

12 Cut off and discard the root ends of the onions, and slice them. Place them in a small airtight container.

13 Prepare the marinade for the steak by combining in a container 2 tablespoons of soy sauce, 2 tablespoons of sunflower oil, the 6 sprigs of coriander (chopped), 1 tablespoon of sliced spring onions, one-third of the ginger (grated), and ½ teaspoon of chopped garlic. Place the skirt steaks into the marinade.

14 Chop the remaining ginger. Place the remaining chopped garlic and chopped ginger into a small airtight container.

15 Wash the cucumbers and cut them into rounds. Slice the tomatoes. Place the sliced cucumbers and tomatoes into a container with the beans (the beans will be protected by their skins).

It's all done! Leave to cool.

Place in the refrigerator:
* The marinated fennel (keeps for 2 days)
* The turkey cordon bleus (keeps for 2 days)
* The marinated steak (keeps for 3 days)
* The carrot purée (keeps for 3 days)
* The stuffed pasta shells, in their baking dish, covered with clingfilm (keeps for 4 days)
* The hard-boiled eggs (keeps for 5 days)
* The container containing the tomatoes, cucumbers and beans (keeps for 1 week)
* The sliced spring onions (keeps for 1 week)
* The rinsed lettuce (keeps for 1 week)
* The grated carrots (keeps for 1 week)
* The remaining coriander (keeps for 1 week)
* The small container containing the garlic and chopped ginger (keeps for 1 week)
* The vinaigrette (keeps for 1 week)

Place in the freezer:
* The slices of baguette (if necessary)

16 Cut the mozzarella ball into 8 slices. Arrange the 3 shallow bowls. In the first bowl, add 25g flour. In the second bowl, add 3 eggs, lightly beaten. In the third bowl, add 100g of dried breadcrumbs.

17 Prepare the turkey cordon bleu. Place 1 turkey steak between 2 rectangular sheets of clingfilm. Using the bottom of a saucepan, firmly pound on the steak to flatten it out. Repeat for each steak. Cut the slices of ham in half. Place 1 ham half on top of each turkey steak. Place 2 slices of mozzarella on top in the centre. Season with salt and pepper. Fold the steak over onto itself to close it. Dredge both sides of the cutlet in the flour, shaking off any excess, then dip it into the eggs. Press both sides into the dried breadcrumbs to coat. Repeat these steps for each steak, then transfer them to a container.

18 Make a vinaigrette by combining 2 tablespoons of mustard, 3 tablespoons of vinegar, 1 teaspoon of salt and a little pepper. Vigorously whisk the mixture while slowly drizzling in 6 tablespoons of olive oil, 1 tablespoon at a time, until smooth.

19 If you purchased the baguette over the weekend, slice it, and place the slices into the freezer bag.

Menu #3

Monday

Starter
Fennel marinated in olive oil and lemon

Main
Turkey cordon bleu

Cooking time:
10 minutes

Ingredients: the marinated fennel, olive oil, turkey cordon bleus, half the lettuce leaves, vinaigrette
Remove the marinated fennel from the refrigerator at least 15 minutes before serving.
In a frying pan, heat 3 tablespoons of olive oil until warm. Cook the turkey cordon bleus for 5 minutes on each side over low heat, or until the turkey is cooked through.
Serve with the fennel and lettuce leaves dressed with the vinaigrette (reserving some of the vinaigrette for the following days).

Reheating time:
10 minutes
Cooking time:
5 minutes

Tuesday

Marinated skirt steak, puréed baby carrots

Ingredients: the carrot purée, sliced spring onions, marinated skirt steak
Reheat the carrot purée in a saucepan or in the microwave. Sprinkle 1 tablespoon of the sliced spring onions over the top. Cook the skirt steaks in their marinade for 5 minutes over high heat, or until cooked to your liking.

Wednesday

Spinach and ricotta stuffed shells

Reheating time:
10 minutes

Ingredients: the stuffed pasta shells, Parmesan
Preheat the oven to 220°C/gas mark 7. Sprinkle the shells with the Parmesan, and bake for 10 minutes, or until browned on top.

Thursday

Salad Niçoise

Preparation time:
10 minutes
Cooking time:
10 minutes

Ingredients: the quick-cook grains; the container with the tomatoes, cucumber and beans; the hard-boiled eggs, anchovies; the tuna, drained; 4 sprigs of coriander; the sliced spring onions; olives; vinaigrette

Cook the grains according to the packet instructions. Rinse under cold water to cool. Remove the skins from the beans by pinching them between your fingers. Peel the hard-boiled eggs. Combine all the ingredients in a large bowl, and serve with some of the vinaigrette (reserve a little of the vinaigrette for the next day).

Cooking time:
10 minutes
Preparation time:
15 minutes

Friday

Starter
Warm goats' cheese toasts

Main
Prawn pad thai

Ingredients: the baguette, goats' cheese, dried thyme, remaining lettuce leaves, remaining vinaigrette, the rice noodles, frozen prawns, sunflower oil, garlic-ginger mixture, grated carrots, soy sauce, fish sauce, 3 eggs, bean sprouts, remaining spring onions, remaining coriander, lime wedges

Preheat the oven to 220°C/gas mark 7. Slice the baguette. Toast the slices in the oven for 3 minutes. Cut the goats' cheese log into rounds. Place 1 goats' cheese round onto each slice of toasted bread, sprinkle with thyme and return to the oven for 3 more minutes to melt the cheese. Serve the toasts on top of the lettuce leaves dressed with the vinaigrette. Place the noodles in very hot water for 5 minutes to rehydrate. Rinse and dry the prawns, then score each down the back using a sharp paring knife. Heat 3 tablespoons of sunflower oil in a wok or sauté pan. Add the prawns, and let them cook for 1 minute over very high heat. Remove the prawns from the pan and place them in a bowl. Add the garlic-ginger mixture to the wok. Cook for 1 minute. Add the grated carrots, 4 tablespoons of soy sauce and 4 tablespoons of fish sauce. Add the drained rehydrated noodles and about 200ml water. Cook for 5 minutes, stirring frequently. Move the noodles to the side of the pan, and break the 3 eggs into the bottom of the pan next to the noodles. Cook for 2 minutes, then stir to combine the cooked eggs into the noodles. Add the prawns back to the pan, stir for 30 seconds, then turn off the heat. Add the bean sprouts and spring onions, and sprinkle with chopped coriander. Serve with lime wedges.

Menu #4

Fruit / Vegetables

* 1.8kg new potatoes
* 250g small green peas, shelled
* 200g mangetouts
* 3 carrots
* 1 small head of cauliflower
* 1 small head of broccoli
* 1 bunch of chives
* 1 bunch of chervil
* 6 green asparagus spears
* 3½ oz (100g) baby spinach
* 2 organic lemons
* 3 onions
* 4 garlic cloves

Basics

* 2 bay leaves
* Ras el hanout
* Ground cumin
* Olive oil
* Salt, black pepper

Meat / Fish

* 1 bone-in veal chop (about 1kg)
* 300g smoked mackerel fillets
* 400g boneless, skinless chicken breasts

Refrigerator

* 125g unsalted butter
* 330ml double cream
* 300g fromage frais
* 170g feta cheese

Store cupboard

* 250g tagliatelle
* 8 slices white sandwich bread
* 1 (425g) can chickpeas
* 200g bulgur wheat
* 250g white rice
* 4 tbsp capers, drained
* Wine vinegar
* 100g almonds
* 2 (400g) cans chopped tomatoes
* 30g pitted black olives
* 2 chicken stock cubes

Monday

Pot-roast veal with spring vegetables

Tuesday

Starter
Cauliflower in caper vinaigrette

Main
Savoury cheesecake

Wednesday

Starter
Smoked mackerel rillettes

Main
Chicken puttanesca

Thursday

Spiced bulgur with cauliflower, broccoli and chickpeas

Friday

Smoked mackerel tagliatelle and vegetables

Menu #4

Set up

If you have enough work space, set out all the ingredients needed for this cooking session. This includes everything except 1 lemon, the cream, tagliatelle, 4 slices of white sandwich bread, chickpeas, bulgur and rice. This allows you to have everything at your fingertips and to not lose time searching for the ingredients in the store cupboard or refrigerator.

Set out the necessary equipment:

* 1 lidded cast-iron casserole or stockpot
* 1 sauté pan
* 1 large baking dish
* 1 (20cm) removable-bottom flat tin
* 1 food processor
* 1 mixing bowl
* 1 salad spinner (or a large bowl and clean tea towel)
* 1 small grater or zester (for the lemon zest)
* 2 small bowls
* 6 containers: 3 large + 1 medium + 2 small
* 1 small lidded glass jar
* Baking paper, clingfilm

Everything is now ready for a cooking time of 1 hour 55 minutes.

1 Preheat the oven to 180°C/gas mark 4. Place 4 slices of the sandwich bread and the almonds in the large baking dish. Bake for 10 minutes, or until golden. Remove the bread and almonds, and set them aside. Leave the oven on.

2 Peel the onions and garlic cloves. Thinly slice them, and place them in 2 separate bowls.

3 In the cast-iron casserole, heat 3 tablespoons of olive oil until warm. Season the veal rib on both sides with salt and pepper, and cook it over high heat until browned, about 5 minutes on each side.

4 Remove the veal rib from the pan, and add one-third of the sliced onions and garlic to the pan along with 1 teaspoon of salt. Cook for 5 minutes over low heat, or until slightly softened.

5 Meanwhile, peel the potatoes and carrots. Cut the carrots into thick rounds and cut the potatoes in half. Place the potatoes and carrots in the pan. Add 200ml water, 1 chicken stock cube and the bay leaves. Place the veal rib back in the pan, cover, and cook gently over a low heat for 20 minutes.

6 In the large baking dish, place the chopped tomatoes, black olives, half the remaining garlic and onions, and 2 tablespoons of the capers. Drizzle everything with 3 tablespoons of olive oil, season with salt and pepper, and stir briefly to coat. Bake for 35 minutes.

7 In the food processor, place the toasted bread and half the toasted almonds. Process until the mixture is reduced to fine crumbs. Melt the butter. Add three-quarters of the melted butter to the food processor and process briefly to combine. Set the remaining butter aside.

8 Cut out a circle of baking paper the diameter of the bottom of the flat tin. Place the paper circle on the bottom of the tin, and cover it with the toasted bread and almond mixture. Using the bottom of a drinking glass, gently press the mixture down into the tin, allowing the mixture to rise up the sides of the tin. Place the tin in the refrigerator.

9 Wash the bowl of the food processor to prepare the rillettes. In the food processor, place half (150g) of the mackerel fillets (skinned), 100g of the fromage

Steps

Menu #4

frais, the remaining melted butter, and the zest of 1 lemon and two-thirds of its juice. Process briefly to combine.

10 Wash the chives and chervil and gently dry them in the salad spinner, or pat them dry using the clean tea towel. Chop one-third of the chives and sprinkle them over the mackerel mixture (rillettes). Stir to combine, and place the mixture in the serving bowl.

11 To the casserole, add the mangetouts and half the shelled green peas, and cook for a further 15 minutes, or until the veal is cooked through.

12 Slice the chicken breasts, add the slices to the large baking dish, and stir to combine. Continue baking for 10 more minutes, or until the chicken is cooked through.

13 Wash the food processor to prepare the savoury cheesecake. In the food processor, place the remaining fromage frais, half the feta and the remaining juice of the lemon. Process until well combined, then transfer the mixture to the mixing bowl. Chop half the remaining chives and stir them into the mixture using a spatula. Remove the flat tin from the refrigerator, and spread the cream cheese mixture over the bottom of the tin.

It's all done! Leave to cool.

Place in the refrigerator:
* The raw green vegetables: the remaining peas, the baby spinach and the peeled asparagus spears
* The veal chop, in its pan
* Half the cooked cauliflower, without the cooking water (keeps for 4 days)
* The cooked broccoli and cauliflower in their cooking water (keeps for 4 days)
* The smoked mackerel rillettes (keeps for 5 days)
* The savoury cheesecake (keeps for 3 days)
* The remaining chives and chervil (keeps for 1 week)
* The caper vinaigrette (keeps for 1 week)
* The remaining smoked mackerel, loosely wrapped
* The remaining feta, loosely wrapped

Place in the freezer:
* The chicken puttanesca, preferably in its baking dish, wrapped in clingfilm
* Store cupboard:
* The toasted almonds

14 Wash the baby spinach and dry the leaves in the salad spinner (or fill a large bowl with water and wash the leaves, then gently pat them dry with the tea towel). Top the baking dish with half the baby spinach, and continue baking for 2 more minutes, or until the leaves are wilted.

15 In the sauté pan, heat 2 tablespoons of olive oil until warm. Add the remaining chopped onions, 1 tablespoon of the ras el hanout and ½ teaspoon of salt. Cook for 5 minutes over low heat. Cut the broccoli and cauliflower into florets, and add them to the sauté pan with the remaining stock cube. Add just enough water to cover the vegetables, and cook, covered, for 15 minutes.

16 Prepare the caper vinaigrette. Combine 4 tablespoons of olive oil, 2 tablespoons of wine vinegar, ½ teaspoon of cumin and the remaining capers. Season with salt and pepper.

17 Using a knife, roughly chop the remaining toasted almonds. Set them aside in the small glass jar.

18 Peel the asparagus, cut off and discard the tough stem end, cut the asparagus crossways in half, then cut the sections lengthways in half.

Menu #4

Menu #4

Monday

Pot-roast veal with spring vegetables

Reheating time:
15 minutes

Ingredients: the pan with the veal and vegetables, salt and pepper
Reheat the veal and vegetables for 15 minutes over medium heat. Season with salt and pepper, and serve.

Cooking time:
5 minutes
Preparation time:
3 minutes

Tuesday

Starter
Cauliflower in caper vinaigrette

Main
Savoury cheesecake

Ingredients: the caper vinaigrette, cooked cauliflower, 4 sprigs of chives, the container with the raw green vegetables, 4 sprigs of chervil, savoury cheesecake
Pour the vinaigrette over the cauliflower, top with chopped chives and stir to combine. Serve.
Bring a saucepan of salted water to a boil. Cook half the asparagus pieces and half the green peas in the boiling water for 5 minutes; they should remain somewhat firm. Chop the chervil and sprinkle it over the cheesecake for garnish. Serve with the cooked peas and asparagus and some of the baby spinach. Place the remaining raw vegetables in the refrigerator to serve on Friday.
For Wednesday, remove the chicken puttanesca from the freezer and defrost it in the refrigerator.

Wednesday

Starter
Smoked mackerel rillettes

Main
Chicken puttanesca

Reheating time:
10 minutes
Cooking time:
15 minutes
Preparation time:
5 minutes

Ingredients: the 4 remaining slices of sandwich bread, smoked mackerel rillettes, 4 sprigs of chervil, chicken puttanesca, rice
Toast the bread in a toaster. Cut the toasts into quarters. Spread the smoked mackerel rillettes on top of the toast pieces, sprinkle them with chopped chervil and serve.
Preheat the oven to 180°C/gas mark 4. Reheat the chicken puttanesca for 10 minutes. Cook the rice according to the packet instructions, and serve alongside the chicken.

Thursday

Cooking time:
10 minutes
Reheating time:
5 minutes
Preparation time:
3 minutes

Spiced bulgur with cauliflower, broccoli and chickpeas

Ingredients: the bulgur, the can of chickpeas, cooked broccoli and cauliflower with their liquid, toasted almonds, half the remaining chives and chervil

Cook the bulgur according to the packet instructions (in general about 10 minutes in boiling salted water). Drain and rinse the chickpeas. Add the chickpeas to the container with the broccoli and cauliflower. Reheat for 5 minutes in the microwave. Spoon the broccoli, cauliflower and chickpeas over the bulgur. Sprinkle with the toasted almonds. Chop the herbs and sprinkle them over the top.

Cooking time:
15 minutes
Preparation time:
10 minutes

Friday

Smoked mackerel tagliatelle and vegetables

Ingredients: the tagliatelle, remaining raw green vegetables, remaining smoked mackerel, 1 lemon, remaining feta, remaining fresh herbs, the cream, salt and pepper

Bring a large saucepan of salted water to a boil. Cook the tagliatelle in boiling water with the asparagus and peas. Two minutes before the end of the cooking time, add the baby spinach.

Meanwhile, slice the smoked mackerel. Zest and juice the lemon. Dice the feta into small cubes. Chop the fresh herbs. Drain the pasta and vegetables and add them to a large bowl. Add the cream, the lemon zest and juice, the mackerel slices, the diced feta and the chopped fresh herbs to the bowl. Season with salt and pepper, stir to combine, then serve.

Summer

Menu #1

Menu #1

Menu #1

Fruit / Vegetables

* 4 large, or 8 medium, round tomatoes, for stuffing
* 4 on-the-vine tomatoes
* 6 courgettes
* 1 aubergine
* 5 red peppers
* 3 large potatoes
* 1 cucumber
* 1 lemon
* 1 bunch of fresh coriander
* 1 bunch of basil
* 6 garlic cloves
* 4 onions

Meat / Fish

* 4 chicken legs
* 400g minced veal (or beef)
* 8 slices cured ham of your choice* (such as Parma ham)

Refrigerator

* 170g crème fraîche or natural yogurt
* 1 small round goats' cheese (about 60g)
* 170g feta cheese
* 150g grated mozzarella cheese
* 2 balls pizza dough (about 400g each)
* 1 sheet of ready-rolled pastry (about 225g)

Basics

* Herbes de Provence
* Wine vinegar
* Olive oil
* Salt, black pepper

Store cupboard

* 150g pitted black olives
* 250g white rice
* 150g white quinoa
* 440ml passata
* 450g short pasta (such as penne)

Monday

Starter
Quinoa tabbouleh

Main
Chicken legs and
ratatouille

Tuesday

Prosciutto* and
vegetable pizza

Wednesday

Courgette, olive and
chicken pasta

Thursday

Starter
Goats' cheese and
ratatouille turnovers

Main
Stuffed tomatoes and rice

Friday

Family-size vegetable
pasta salad

*For a pork-free menu, replace the prosciutto with turkey breast.

Set up

If you have enough work space, set out all the ingredients needed for this cooking session. This includes everything except the ham, puff pastry (keep refrigerated until right before using), pizza dough, feta, mozzarella, olives, rice, passata and pasta. This allows you to have everything at your fingertips and to not lose time searching for the ingredients in the store cupboard or refrigerator.

Set out the necessary equipment:

* 1 baking sheet
* 1 large saucepan
* 1 frying pan
* 1 lidded cast-iron casserole or stockpot
* 2 small bowls
* 1 gratin dish (or shallow baking dish)
* 1 salad spinner (or clean tea towel)
* 1 sieve
* 1 drinking glass 8–10cm in diameter
* 10 containers: 3 small + 5 medium + 2 large
* Kitchen paper, baking paper

Everything is now ready for a cooking time of 1½ hours.

1 Preheat the oven to 220°C/gas mark 7.

2 Peel all of the onions and garlic cloves and cut them into small dice. Divide them individually between the 2 small bowls.

3 Arrange the chicken legs on the baking sheet lined with baking paper. Sprinkle the chicken generously with the herbes de Provence. Season with salt. Bake for 40 minutes, or until cooked through.

4 Prepare the ratatouille. In the cast-iron casserole, heat 2 tablespoons of olive oil until warm. Add half

the diced onions and garlic, then add 1 tablespoon of salt. Cook gently until slightly softened.

5 Meanwhile, wash the peppers, cut them in half, remove and discard the seeds and white membrane, and cut into small dice. Add 3 of the diced peppers to the pan. Place the remaining peppers in an airtight container, and refrigerate.

6 Wash the courgettes. Cut off and discard the ends, and cut the courgettes into small dice. Add 3 of the diced courgettes to the pan. Place the remaining diced courgettes in an airtight container, and refrigerate.

7 Wash the tomatoes for stuffing. Cut off the tops and set them aside. Using a spoon, scoop out the flesh of the tomatoes and add it to the pan.

Season inside the tomatoes with salt, and place them upside down on a plate lined with kitchen paper to drain any excess liquid.

8 Wash the aubergine, cut it into small dice, and add it to the pan.

9 Peel the potatoes, cut them into small dice, and add them to the pan. Cover the pot, and simmer for 35 minutes, stirring occasionally.

10 Place the basil and coriander in the salad spinner, then wash and gently dry them (or rinse under cool water and dry with the clean tea towel). Place all of the basil and half the coriander in an airtight container between 2 sheets of kitchen paper. Place the container in the refrigerator for up to 1 week.

Steps

11 Prepare the stuffing for the tomatoes. In the frying pan, heat 1 tablespoon of olive oil until warm. Add the remaining diced onions, half the remaining garlic and 1 teaspoon of salt. Cook for 5 minutes, or until slightly softened. Meanwhile, chop the remaining coriander. Add the minced veal and the coriander to the pan. Cook for 10 minutes, stirring frequently.

12 Bring 1.5 litres of salted water to a boil in the large saucepan. Thoroughly rinse the quinoa.

13 Peel the cucumber and cut it into small dice. Wash the on-the-vine tomatoes, and cut them into small dice. Store the cucumber and tomatoes separately in airtight containers (to serve with the salads).

14 Cook the quinoa in the boiling water for 15 minutes, or until tender.

15 Fill the tomatoes with the stuffing mixture, and place them in the baking dish. Replace the tops, and bake for 30 minutes, or until somewhat shrivelled and the meat is cooked through. Remove the chicken from the oven at the same time, and leave to cool.

16 Spoon 6 tablespoons of the ratatouille into the sieve, and press down with the back of a spoon to release as much liquid as possible; set aside.

17 Prepare the lemon sauce for the tabbouleh. Combine the juice from the lemon with 2 tablespoons of olive oil, ½ teaspoon of salt and a little pepper.

It's all done! Leave to cool.

Place in the refrigerator:
* The cooked quinoa (keeps for 2 days)
* The lemon sauce for the quinoa tabbouleh (keeps for 3 days)
* The containers of raw vegetables: peppers, courgettes, tomatoes and cucumber (keeps for 1 week)
* The ratatouille, in its pan (keeps for 3 days)
* The 2 whole chicken legs, in an airtight container (keeps for 2 days)
* The basil and coriander, in an airtight container (keeps for 1 week)
* The remaining garlic, in a small airtight container (keeps for 1 week)

Place in the freezer:
* The goats' cheese and ratatouille turnovers
* The stuffed tomatoes
* The shredded chicken meat

18 Unroll the puff pastry sheet. Cut out 9 (10cm) circles using the rim of the drinking glass. Cut the goats' cheese into small dice. Spoon some of the goats' cheese into the centre of each pastry circle. Top the goats' cheese with 2 teaspoons of the drained ratatouille, and sprinkle the top with herbes de Provence. Fold one side of each pastry circle over the filling to form a turnover. Seal the edges by gently pressing them with the tines of a fork. Bake for 20 minutes, or until golden and flaky.

19 Drain the quinoa and rinse it under cold water. Place it in an airtight container.

20 Shred the flesh of 2 of the chicken legs, and set it aside in an airtight container.

Each night's prep

Menu #1

Monday

Starter
Quinoa tabbouleh

Main
Chicken legs and ratatouille

Reheating time:
15 minutes
Preparation time:
2 minutes

Ingredients: the pan of ratatouille, the whole chicken legs, half the coriander, the cooked quinoa, containers of diced tomatoes, the cucumber and peppers, lemon sauce

Reheat the ratatouille in its pan, and reheat the chicken legs either in the oven preheated to 180°C/gas mark 4 or in the pan with the ratatouille.

Chop the coriander. In a large bowl, combine the quinoa, coriander, half the containers of diced tomatoes and cucumber, and a quarter of the diced peppers. Pour the lemon sauce over the top, and stir to combine. Serve.

Cooking time:
10 minutes
Preparation time:
6 minutes

Tuesday

Prosciutto and vegetable pizza

Ingredients: the 2 balls of pizza dough, the passata, the container of courgettes and peppers, a little of the herbes de Provence, a few black olives (optional), the grated mozzarella, the ham slices (or turkey) and 2 sprigs of basil

Preheat the oven to 220°C/gas mark 7. Meanwhile, roll out the pizza dough and cover each dough circle with some of the passata, leaving a 2cm border. Divide half the courgettes and half the peppers and distribute them on top (place the remaining in the refrigerator). Sprinkle with herbes de Provence and distribute several black olives, if using, on top. Top with the shredded mozzarella. Bake for 10 minutes, then place 4 slices of the ham and several basil leaves on top. Serve.
For Wednesday, remove the shredded chicken meat from the freezer and defrost it in the refrigerator.

<u>**Cooking and reheating time:**</u>
15 minutes
<u>**Preparation time:**</u>
2 minutes

<u>Wednesday</u>

Courgette, olive and chicken pasta

Ingredients: the pasta, olive oil, remaining garlic, the container of courgettes, the defrosted shredded chicken meat, crème fraîche, 1 handful of black olives, half the basil, salt and pepper

Cook the pasta in a large saucepan filled with salted water. Meanwhile, heat 1 tablespoon of olive oil in a sauté pan until warm. Add the garlic and all of the courgettes. Cook for 10 minutes, or until softened. Drain the pasta. Set aside half the pasta in an airtight container (for the pasta salad on Friday). To the sauté pan, add the chicken meat, crème fraîche, olives and pasta. Season with salt and pepper. Cook for 2 minutes. Sprinkle with basil. Serve.

<u>For Thursday, remove the goats' cheese and ratatouille turnovers and the stuffed tomatoes from the freezer and defrost them in the refrigerator.</u>

<u>Thursday</u>

<u>**Reheating time:**</u>
15 minutes
<u>**Cooking time:**</u>
10 minutes

Starter
Goats' cheese and ratatouille turnovers

Main
Stuffed tomatoes and rice

Ingredients: the goats' cheese and ratatouille turnovers, stuffed tomatoes, rice

Reheat the turnovers and the stuffed tomatoes in the oven preheated to 160°C/gas mark 3. Cook the rice according to the packet instructions. Serve.

<u>**Preparation time:**</u>
5 minutes

<u>Friday</u>

Family-size vegetable pasta salad

Ingredients: the feta, remaining coriander and basil, the cooked pasta, the container of cucumber and peppers, remaining black olives, olive oil, wine vinegar, salt and pepper

Dice the feta. Chop the coriander and basil. Place all the ingredients in a large bowl. Drizzle with 2 tablespoons of olive oil and 1 tablespoon of vinegar.
Season with salt and pepper, and toss to combine. Serve.

Menu #2

Menu #2

Shopping list

Menu #2

Fruit / Vegetables

* 4 large aubergines
* 4 courgettes
* 1.5kg large Charlotte (or waxy) potatoes
* 500g green beans (fresh or frozen)
* 250g white button mushrooms
* 500 g shelled peas (fresh or frozen)
* 1 cucumber
* 1 small container of assorted cherry tomatoes (about 170g)
* 1 bunch of spring onions
* 1 small bag baby salad leaves (about 140g)
* 1 bunch of mint
* 1 bunch of dill
* 1 lemon
* 3 garlic cloves
* 2 red onions

Basics

* 180g dried breadcrumbs
* Whole nutmeg
* Wine vinegar
* Olive oil
* Salt, black pepper

Meat / Fish

* 1kg minced beef
* 4 fresh skinless salmon fillets
* 2 fresh cod loins (300g total)

Refrigerator

* 25g unsalted butter
* 330ml double cream
* 170g feta cheese
* 250g ricotta cheese
* 60g grated Parmesan cheese
* 4 large eggs

Store cupboard

* 400g green lentils
* 250g white or brown rice
* 1 (400g) can chopped tomatoes
* 270ml passata
* Ground cinnamon

Monday

Family-size potato, salmon, mixed leaf, onion and cucumber salad

Tuesday

Starter
Greek lentil salad

Main
Stuffed courgettes

Wednesday

Moussaka

Thursday

Fish stew with dill and rice

Friday

Starter
Pea, feta and mint soup

Main
Lentil balls in tomato sauce with green beans

Steps
Menu #2

Set up

If you have enough work space, set out all the ingredients needed for this cooking session. This includes everything except the green beans, cherry tomatoes, salad leaves, lemon, passata and rice. This allows you to have everything at your fingertips and to not lose time searching for the ingredients in the store cupboard or refrigerator. Set out the necessary equipment:

* 2 baking sheets
* 2 small bowls
* 1 steam cooker or lidded saucepan with a steam basket
* 1 large baking dish
* 1 sauté pan
* 1 large saucepan
* 1 small frying pan
* 1 food processor
* 1 stick blender
* 1 sieve
* 1 salad spinner (or large bowl and clean tea towel)
* 1 (1.5-litre) glass jar (for storing the pea soup)
* 6 containers: 3 large + 3 medium
* Kitchen paper, baking paper, clingfilm

Everything is now ready for a cooking time of 2 hours.

1 Preheat the oven to 220°C/gas mark 7. Wash the aubergines, cut them lengthways into strips 2cm thick. Place the strips on the two baking sheets lined with baking paper. Brush them with a little olive oil and season with salt. Bake for 30 minutes, or until somewhat shrivelled and lightly browned.

2 Wash the courgettes. Cut them lengthways in half. Using a small spoon, scoop out the flesh from the centres. Place the hollowed halves in the oven next to the aubergines, and bake for 10 minutes.

3 Soak the mint and dill in water for 5 minutes, then spin them dry in the salad spinner (or dry with the tea towel). Place half the mint and dill in an airtight

container between 2 sheets of kitchen paper. Refrigerate for up to 1 week. Chop the remaining mint and dill and place each separately in the small bowls.

<u>4</u> Peel the potatoes. Steam them for about 20 minutes, or until tender when pierced with a fork. Peel the red onions and cut them in half. Cut 3 onion halves into small dice, and the remaining half into thin slices.

<u>5</u> Fill the large saucepan with salted water and bring it to a boil. Meanwhile, peel and finely chop the garlic cloves. Set them aside. Rinse the lentils in the sieve. Cook the lentils in the saucepan of boiling water according to the packet instructions. Do not salt them until the end of the cooking time. Drain, and leave to cool.

<u>6</u> In the sauté pan, heat 2 tablespoons of olive oil until warm. Add two-thirds of the diced red onions and half the chopped garlic. Season with salt and pepper, then cook for 5 minutes, or until slightly softened.

<u>7</u> Meanwhile, peel the cucumber and cut it into small dice. Set it aside in an airtight container.

<u>8</u> To the sauté pan, add two-thirds of the minced beef, and cook for 10 minutes. Using the remaining minced beef, prepare the stuffing for the courgettes. Combine the meat with 1 egg, 4 tablespoons of dried breadcrumbs, half the remaining chopped garlic and red onions and 2 tablespoons of chopped mint. Season with salt and pepper.

9 Fill the pre-cooked courgettes with the stuffing mixture. Sprinkle the tops with half the grated Parmesan, and bake for 15 minutes, or until the meat is cooked through.

10 To the sauté pan, add the chopped tomatoes, ¼ teaspoon of cinnamon and a little salt. Cook gently for 20 minutes.

11 Cut a quarter of the steamed potatoes into rounds, and cut the remaining into large dice.

12 Prepare the topping for the moussaka. Combine half the ricotta cheese with 2 eggs, 50g of the feta (crumbled) and 2 tablespoons of the remaining grated Parmesan.

13 In the baking dish, place one-third of the aubergine strips and all of the potato slices in a single layer. Top with half the tomato and minced beef mixture, then a second third of the aubergine slices, then the remaining meat mixture. Layer the remaining aubergine slices on top, and pour the topping for the moussaka over. Bake for 25 minutes, or until golden on top.

14 Rinse the spring onions, cut off and discard the root ends, strip off the first layer of skin, then chop the onions. Briefly wash the mushrooms, cut off and discard the stems, then cut the tops in half.

15 Rinse and wipe out the sauté pan. In the pan, melt the butter. Add half the chopped spring onions, the mushrooms, and ½ teaspoon of salt. Cook gently for 2 minutes. Add the chopped dill, double

It's all done! Leave to cool.

Place in the refrigerator:
* The diced cucumber (keeps for 1 week)
* The container with the remaining cooked lentils and the red onion slices
* The container with the diced potatoes, salmon and spring onions (keeps for 2 days)
* The stuffed courgettes, if you serve them within 2 days of preparing them
* The mint and fresh dill in an airtight container (keeps for 1 week)

Place in the freezer:
* The stuffed courgettes, if you will serve them more than 2 days after preparing them
* The soup
* The lentil balls
* The moussaka, in its baking dish, covered with clingfilm
* The fish stew

cream, a handful of the peas and 50ml of water to the sauté pan. Cook over gentle heat for 5 minutes.

__16__ Meanwhile, cut the cod and salmon into large dice. Add the fish to the sauté pan, and cook with the cream and vegetables for 5 more minutes.

__17__ Prepare the lentil balls: In the food processor, place half the cooked lentils, the remaining ricotta cheese, 1 egg, the remaining garlic and diced red onions, 125g of the dried breadcrumbs, and 1 tablespoon of the chopped mint. Season with salt and pepper. Process to combine. Using your hands, form the mixture into balls. Roll them in a little of the remaining dried breadcrumbs. In the frying pan, heat 1 tablespoon of olive oil until warm. Cook the lentil balls for 10 minutes, browning them on all sides.

__18__ Meanwhile, bring 1 litre of salted water to a simmer. Place the remaining cooked lentils in an airtight container with the red onion slices.

__19__ Add the remaining peas and half the remaining chopped spring onions to the simmering water. Cook for 15 minutes, then add 1 handful of the diced potatoes, the remaining chopped mint and 40g of the feta. Blend thoroughly using the stick blender, then strain. Transfer the mixture to the glass jar, leaving a little room at the top.

__20__ In the sauté pan with the fish stew, remove half the diced salmon. Place it in a large container with the remaining diced potatoes and the remaining chopped spring onions.

POUR
VENDREDI

Menu #2

Monday

Family-size potato, salmon, mixed leaf, onion and cucumber salad

Preparation time:
5 minutes

Ingredients: the lemon, olive oil, the container with the diced potatoes, salmon and spring onions, the bag of baby salad leaves, half the diced cucumber, half the remaining dill, salt and pepper
Prepare the sauce. In a large bowl, vigorously whisk together the juice of the lemon with 3 tablespoons of olive oil, ½ teaspoon of salt and a pinch of pepper. Add the remaining ingredients and toss to coat. Serve.
For Tuesday, if you have frozen the stuffed courgettes, remove them from the freezer and defrost them in the refrigerator.

Reheating time:
15 minutes
Preparation time:
10 minutes

Tuesday

Starter
Greek lentil salad

Main
Stuffed courgettes

Ingredients: the stuffed courgettes, olive oil, vinegar, cherry tomatoes, cooked lentils with the red onion slices, remaining cucumber, remaining feta, the mint, salt and pepper
Reheat the stuffed courgettes in the oven preheated to 160°C/gas mark 3. In a large bowl, vigorously whisk together 3 tablespoons of olive oil with 1 tablespoon of vinegar, 1 teaspoon of salt and a pinch of pepper. Cut the cherry tomatoes in half. Dice three-quarters of the remaining feta, and place back in the refrigerator. Chop three-quarters of the mint, and place the rest in the refrigerator. In a large bowl, combine the cherry tomatoes, lentils, red onion slices, diced cucumber, diced feta and half the chopped mint. Sprinkle a little of the mint over the top of the warm stuffed courgettes. Serve.
For Wednesday, remove the moussaka from the freezer and defrost it in the refrigerator.

Reheating time:
15 minutes

Wednesday

Moussaka

Ingredients: the moussaka
Reheat the moussaka in the oven preheated to 160°C/
gas mark 3 and serve.
**For Thursday, remove the fish stew from the freezer
and defrost it in the refrigerator.**

Thursday

Fish stew with dill and rice

Reheating time:
10 minutes
Cooking time:
15 minutes
Preparation time:
3 minutes

Ingredients: the thawed fish stew, rice, remaining dill
Reheat the fish stew in a saucepan over very low heat for
10 minutes. Meanwhile, cook the rice according to the
packet instructions. Sprinkle with dill, and serve.
**For Friday, remove the pea soup and the lentil balls
from the freezer and defrost them in the refrigerator.**

Reheating time:
10 minutes
Cooking time:
15 minutes
Preparation time:
10 minutes

Friday

Starter
Pea, feta and mint soup

Main
Lentil balls in tomato sauce with green beans

Ingredients: the soup, remaining feta, remaining mint, the green
beans, passata, lentil balls, salt and pepper
In a saucepan, reheat the soup. Serve it with the remaining
feta crumbled over the top, a little pepper, and chopped
mint. Bring 1.5 litres of salted water to a boil, and cook the
green beans. In a saucepan, place the passata, and add
½ teaspoon of salt and a pinch of pepper. Cook for
5 minutes, until reduced. Add the lentil balls and heat
through, about 5 more minutes.

Menu #3

Menu #3

Fruit / Vegetables

* 3 aubergines
* 800g large Charlotte (or waxy) potatoes
* 2 red peppers
* 2 yellow peppers
* 2 green peppers
* 4 courgettes
* 170g cherry tomatoes
* 1 small bag rocket (about 140g)
* 1 bunch of fresh coriander
* 1 bunch of basil
* 1 small lemon
* 6 garlic cloves
* 4 onions
* 1 (3cm) knob fresh root ginger

Basics

* Whole nutmeg
* Olive oil
* Salt, black pepper

Meat / Fish

* 8 merguez sausages
* 8 slices bresaola (air-dried salted beef)
* 4 boneless, skinless chicken breasts

Refrigerator

* 6 large eggs
* 1 ball 227g fresh mozzarella cheese
* 250ml double cream

Store cupboard

* 1 large rustic loaf of bread
* 250g spaghetti
* 250g quick-cook grains – such as bulgur
* 250g couscous
* Soy sauce
* Clear honey
* Tahini (optional)
* Ground cumin
* Ground coriander

Monday

Marinated chicken kebabs with wheat and roasted vegetables

Tuesday

Merguez with couscous

Wednesday

Starter
Aubergine caviar

Main
Spanish omelette

Thursday

Summer bruschetta

Friday

Starter
Peppers marinated in garlic and olive oil

Main
Tunisian spaghetti

Steps

Menu #3

Set up

If you have enough work space, set out all the ingredients needed for this cooking session. This includes everything except the rocket, bresaola, mozzarella, spaghetti, grains and couscous. This allows you to have everything at your fingertips and to not lose time searching for the ingredients in the store cupboard or refrigerator. Set out the necessary equipment:

* 2 large baking sheets
* 1 (20cm) round cake tin
* 1 food processor
* 2 large serving bowls
* 1 salad spinner (or large bowl and clean tea towel)
* 1 frying pan
* 4 kebab skewers (optional)
* 1 small grater or zester (for the nutmeg)
* 4 containers: 2 large + 2 medium
* 2 freezer bags
* Kitchen paper, baking paper, clingfilm

Everything is now ready for a cooking time of 1¾ hours.

1 Preheat the grill. Cut the red, yellow and green peppers in half, and remove and discard the seeds and white membranes. On a baking sheet lined with baking paper, place 2 of the whole aubergines and the pepper halves, skin side up. Bake directly under the grill for 30 minutes, or until the skins are nicely browned.

2 Wash and dry the courgettes, the remaining aubergine and the cherry tomatoes. Peel the potatoes. Peel the onions and garlic cloves.

3 Dice the courgettes and the aubergine. Thinly slice the onions and roughly chop the garlic. Cut the potatoes into thin rounds.

4 Place the basil and coriander in the salad spinner (or a large bowl) filled with water. Soak the coriander for 5 minutes. Drain the water, then gently spin the herbs dry (or dry with the tea towel). Place the coriander in an airtight container between 2 sheets of kitchen paper. Refrigerate for up to 1 week.

5 Remove the peppers and aubergines from the oven. Set them aside on a plate to cool.

6 Preheat the oven to 200°C/gas mark 6. Line the 2 baking sheets with baking paper. On one of the lined baking sheets, arrange all of the potato rounds and a quarter of the following ingredients: the courgettes, cherry tomatoes, onions and garlic. On the other baking sheet, place the remaining courgettes, cherry tomatoes, onions and half the chopped garlic. Drizzle 2 tablespoons of olive oil over the vegetables on each baking sheet, season with salt and pepper and stir briefly to coat. Bake for 30 minutes, or until the vegetables are lightly browned.

Menu #3

7 Make the marinade for the chicken. Peel and grate the ginger. In a large container, combine 4 tablespoons of soy sauce, 1 tablespoon of olive oil, 1 tablespoon of honey, the freshly grated ginger and one-third of the remaining garlic. Dice the chicken into equal-sized pieces. Place the diced chicken in the marinade, stir to combine, then transfer it to an airtight container.

8 Prepare the aubergine caviar. Scoop out the flesh of the whole aubergines. Place the flesh in the food processor with half the remaining garlic, the juice of the lemon, 1 tablespoon of tahini (if using), ½ teaspoon of cumin, and 1 tablespoon of olive oil. Process until smooth. Transfer the mixture to a serving dish and cover it with clingfilm.

9 Peel the skins from all the peppers. Cut the flesh into strips. Place the strips of green pepper aside (they will be used for the Tunisian spaghetti). Place half the red and yellow pepper strips in an attractive bowl. Add 3 tablespoons of olive oil, the remaining chopped garlic and 1 teaspoon of salt. Stir to combine, cover with clingfilm, and refrigerate. Dice the remaining strips of red and yellow pepper.

10 In the large bowl, beat the eggs with a whisk. Add the cream. Season with salt and pepper, then add 1 pinch of freshly grated nutmeg.

11 Lower the oven temperature to 180°C/gas mark 4. Grease the bottom and sides of the cake tin. Cut out a circle of baking paper the diameter of the bottom of the tin and place it in the tin.

It's all done! Leave to cool.

Place in the refrigerator:
* The aubergine caviar (keeps for 1 week)
* The marinated peppers (keeps for 1 week)
* The marinated chicken (keeps for 2 days)
* The roasted vegetables with the 4 cooked whole sausages (keeps for 3 days)
* The basil and coriander, in an airtight container (keeps for 1 week)

Place in the freezer:
* The slices of bread
* The Spanish omelette, in its tin, covered with clingfilm
* The container with the slices of green peppers, the cherry tomatoes and the sausages

Distribute the roasted vegetables from the first baking sheet in step 6 in the cake tin, then scrape the egg mixture over the vegetables. Bake for 30 minutes, or until golden on top.

12 Cut 4 of the sausages into 1cm long pieces. Leave the 4 remaining sausages whole. Heat the frying pan without any added fat, and cook the sausage pieces and the whole sausages until cooked through. Remove the whole sausages from the pan and set them aside. To the frying pan, add the strips of green pepper. Cook just until all of the liquid has evaporated. Transfer the cooked mixture from the pan to an airtight container.

13 To the same container, add nearly all of the cherry tomatoes and several of the roasted vegetables.

Store the remaining roasted vegetables with the 4 whole sausages in a large container.

14 Slice the bread. In a freezer bag, place 8 slices from the centre of the loaf (these will be used for the bruschetta), and place the other slices (those sliced nearest the ends of the loaf) in a separate freezer bag (these will be used with the aubergine caviar).

Menu #3

Monday

Marinated chicken kebabs, with wheat and roasted vegetables

Reheating time:
10 minutes
Cooking time:
15 minutes
Preparation time:
1 minute

Ingredients: the quick-cook grains, the marinated chicken, half the roasted vegetables, half the basil, salt and pepper

Cook the grains according to the packet instructions. Reheat the vegetables. Distribute the chicken pieces on 4 skewers (if using). Cook the skewers for 10 minutes in a frying pan (or under the grill). Combine the vegetables and cooked grains. Season and add the basil. Serve with the chicken.

Reheating time:
10 minutes
Cooking time:
15 minutes
Preparation time:
1 minute

Tuesday

Merguez with couscous

Ingredients: the couscous, remaining roasted vegetables with the 4 whole sausages, ½ tsp ground coriander, half the fresh coriander

Cook the couscous according to the packet instructions. In a frying pan without added fat, reheat the sausages and set them aside. In the same pan, place the vegetables, about 125ml of water, and the ground coriander. Cook for 5 minutes. Chop the fresh coriander. Serve the vegetables and sausages with the couscous, sprinkled with coriander.

For Wednesday, remove the omelette and the bag with the bread slices taken from the ends of the loaf from the freezer and defrost them in the refrigerator.

Wednesday

Starter
Aubergine caviar

Main
Spanish omelette

Reheating time:
15 minutes

Ingredients: the omelette, three-quarters of the aubergine caviar, the slices of bread (the bag with the slices taken from the ends of the loaf), 2 sprigs of coriander

Reheat the omelette in the oven preheated to 160°C/gas mark 3. Toast the bread. Serve the toasted bread with the aubergine caviar, sprinkled with chopped coriander. Place the remaining aubergine caviar in the refrigerator to use on Thursday.

For Thursday, remove the bag with the 8 slices of bread from the freezer and defrost them in the refrigerator.

Thursday

Summer bruschetta

Cooking time:
15 minutes
Preparation time:
7 minutes

Ingredients: the 8 slices of bread, mozzarella, remaining aubergine caviar, 16 strips of the marinated peppers, the bresaola, the bag of rocket, 2 sprigs of basil, olive oil

Preheat the oven to 220°C/gas mark 7. Toast the bread in the oven for 4 minutes. Cut the mozzarella into 16 small slices. On each slice of bread, spread 1 tablespoon of aubergine caviar, top with 2 strips of pepper, and 2 slices of mozzarella. Place the toasts in the oven for 1 minute to melt the mozzarella, then top with some of the bresaola, rocket and basil. Drizzle with olive oil.

For Friday, remove the container with the green peppers, cherry tomatoes and sausages from the freezer and defrost it in the refrigerator.

Reheating time:
15 minutes
Cooking time:
15 minutes
Preparation time:
5 minutes

Friday

Starter
Peppers marinated in garlic and olive oil

Main
Tunisian spaghetti

Ingredients: the marinated green peppers, remaining basil; the spaghetti, the container with the thawed green peppers, tomatoes and sausages, the coriander, salt and pepper

Remove the peppers from the marinade, sprinkle with the basil, season with salt and pepper, and serve.
Cook the spaghetti to al dente (still firm to the bite). In a sauté pan, reheat the marinade from the green peppers. Add the vegetable and sausage mixture. Add the cooked spaghetti and sprinkle with the chopped coriander. Toss to combine and serve.

Menu #4

Menu #4

Menu #4

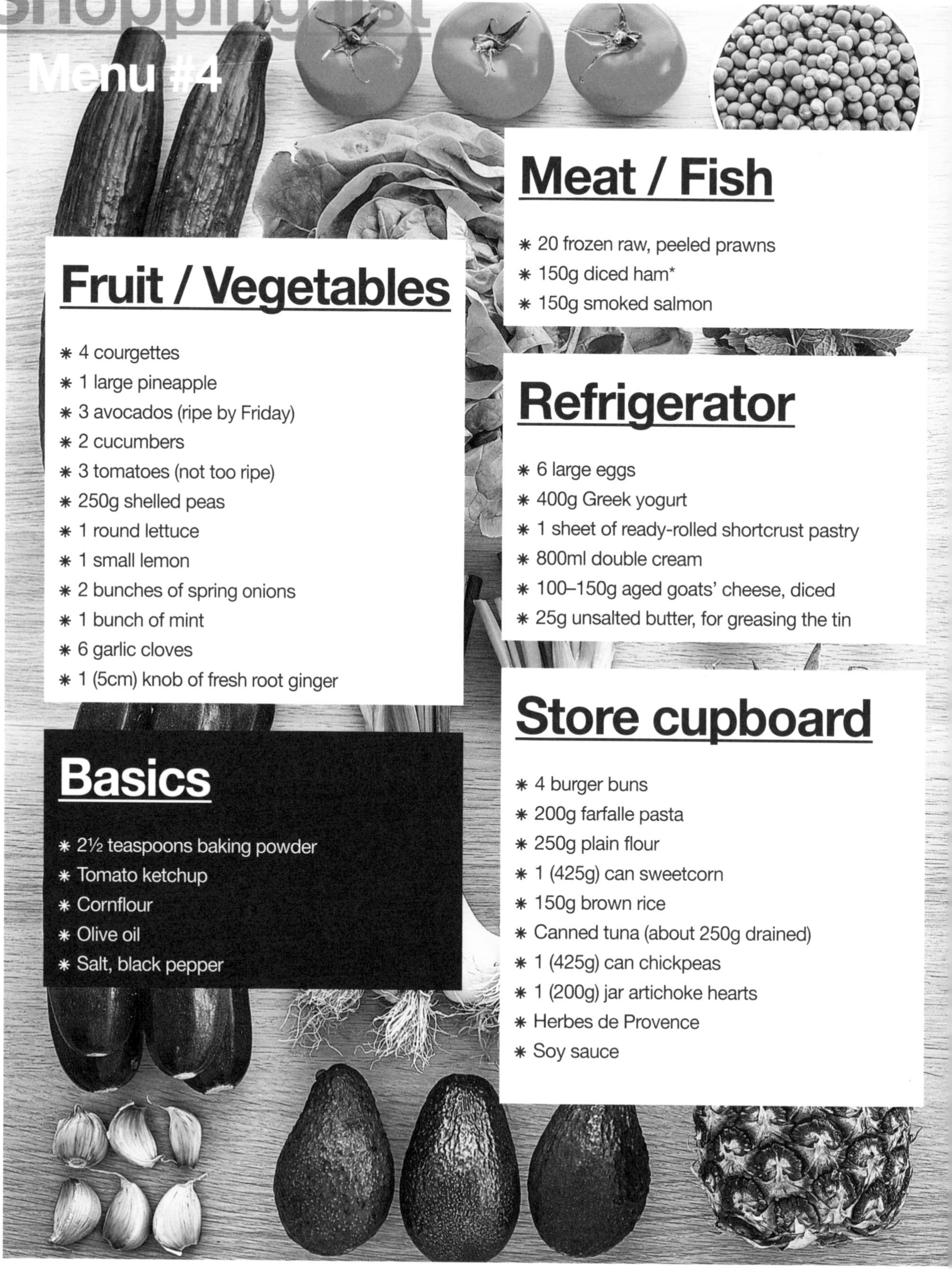

Fruit / Vegetables

* 4 courgettes
* 1 large pineapple
* 3 avocados (ripe by Friday)
* 2 cucumbers
* 3 tomatoes (not too ripe)
* 250g shelled peas
* 1 round lettuce
* 1 small lemon
* 2 bunches of spring onions
* 1 bunch of mint
* 6 garlic cloves
* 1 (5cm) knob of fresh root ginger

Basics

* 2½ teaspoons baking powder
* Tomato ketchup
* Cornflour
* Olive oil
* Salt, black pepper

Meat / Fish

* 20 frozen raw, peeled prawns
* 150g diced ham*
* 150g smoked salmon

Refrigerator

* 6 large eggs
* 400g Greek yogurt
* 1 sheet of ready-rolled shortcrust pastry
* 800ml double cream
* 100–150g aged goats' cheese, diced
* 25g unsalted butter, for greasing the tin

Store cupboard

* 4 burger buns
* 200g farfalle pasta
* 250g plain flour
* 1 (425g) can sweetcorn
* 150g brown rice
* Canned tuna (about 250g drained)
* 1 (425g) can chickpeas
* 1 (200g) jar artichoke hearts
* Herbes de Provence
* Soy sauce

Monday

Starter
Courgette gazpacho

Main
Tuna and tomato quiche

Tuesday

Prawn and pineapple fried rice

Wednesday

Starter
Tzatziki sauce

Main
Courgette and ham loaf*

Thursday

Chickpea burgers

Friday

Farfalle and smoked salmon salad

*For a pork-free menu, replace the ham with turkey breast.

Steps

Set up

If you have enough work space, set out all the ingredients needed for this cooking session. This includes everything except the avocados, 2 tomatoes, the lemon, 1 garlic clove, the frozen prawns, smoked salmon, Greek yogurt, burger buns, sweetcorn and artichoke hearts. This allows you to have everything at your fingertips and to not lose time searching for the ingredients in the store cupboard or refrigerator.

Set out the necessary equipment:
* 1 (20cm) flat tin
* Ceramic baking beans (or dried beans)
* 1 grater with large holes
* 1 colander
* 1 large mixing bowl
* 1 loaf tin
* 1 frying pan
* 1 large saucepan
* 1 food processor
* 1 stick blender
* 1 garlic press (if available)
* 1 salad spinner (or large bowl and clean tea towel)
* 5 containers: 1 large + 2 medium + 2 small
* 1 (1.5-litre) glass jar (for storing the courgette gazpacho)
* Kitchen paper, baking paper, aluminium foil

Everything is now ready for a cooking time of 2 hours 10 minutes.

1 Preheat the oven to 180°C/gas mark 4. Grease the flat tin. Line the tin with the pastry, gently pressing it down into the tin and up the sides. Trim off any excess pastry from around the edges, level with the top of the tin. Prick the base all over with a fork. Crumple the paper included in the packet with the pastry (or use baking paper), place it on top of the pastry in the tin, then fill the tin with the baking beans. Bake the pastry case for 30 minutes, or until pale golden.

2 Peel the cucumbers, halve them lengthways, and scrape out the seeds. Coarsely grate the flesh. Place the grated cucumber in a colander, season

generously with salt, and set aside to drain while you continue cooking.

3 Cut off and discard the root ends of the spring onions, strip off the first layer of skin, thinly slice the onions and place them in a bowl.

4 Prepare the filling for the quiche. In the large mixing bowl, whisk 3 eggs with 1400ml of cream until well combined. Whisk in 1 teaspoon of salt and a little pepper, until combined. Add 2 tablespoons of the sliced spring onions, all of the tuna and one-third of the peas. Wash 1 tomato and slice it into rounds. Scrape the filling into the baked pastry case and top it with the tomato slices. Bake for 45 minutes, or until golden on top, on a shelf positioned near the top of the oven. Wash the mixing bowl.

5 In the large saucepan, bring 500ml of salted water to a boil.

6 Peel 5 of the garlic cloves and press them through a garlic press (or finely chop them). Set them aside in a small bowl. Wash the courgettes. Cut 3 of the courgettes into large dice, and 1 into small dice.

7 To the saucepan of boiling water, add the large pieces of courgette, and cook for 10 minutes.

8 Rinse the lettuce. Detach the leaves and place them in the salad spinner (or large bowl) filled with water. Place any large damaged leaves in the saucepan with the courgettes. Gently spin the leaves dry (or use the tea towel), then place them in the large airtight container between 2 sheets of kitchen paper; the leaves will keep for up to 1 week.

9 Wash and gently dry the mint. Finely chop the entire bunch, and place it in a bowl.

10 In the saucepan with the courgettes, add 2 tablespoons of chopped spring onion, ½ teaspoon chopped garlic, 1 tablespoon of chopped mint and 200ml cream. Blend thoroughly using the stick blender. Transfer the gazpacho to the glass jar.

11 In the frying pan, heat 1 tablespoon of olive oil until warm. Add 2 tablespoons of chopped spring onions, ½ teaspoon of chopped garlic, the small diced courgette and ½ teaspoon of salt. Cook for 10 minutes, uncovered, or until all of the liquid has evaporated. Leave to cool.

12 Prepare the loaf batter. In the large mixing bowl, lightly beat the remaining eggs with 3 tablespoons

of olive oil and the remaining cream. Add the flour a little at a time, then add the baking powder and stir with a whisk to thoroughly combine. Add the diced ham, goats' cheese (diced), 1 tablespoon of chopped mint, the cooked courgette mixture, 1 teaspoon of salt, and 1 tablespoon of herbes de Provence.

Scrape the batter into the greased loaf tin, and bake for 1 hour, or until a cocktail stick inserted in the centre comes out with just a few moist crumbs, on a shelf positioned near the bottom of the oven. After 10 minutes of baking time, make a shallow incision lengthways down the centre of the cake so that it rises evenly.

13 Rinse the brown rice and cook it according to the packet instructions. Drain.

It's all done! Leave to cool.

Place in the refrigerator:
* The remaining chopped spring onions (keeps for 1 week)
* The remaining chopped mint (keeps for 1 week)
* The drained, grated cucumber (keeps for 1 week)
* The rinsed lettuce leaves (keeps for 1 week)
* The courgette gazpacho (keeps for 2 days)
* The tuna quiche in its tin (keeps for 2 days)
* The empty pineapple halves, on a plate covered with foil (keeps for 4 days)
* The fried rice (keeps for 3 days)
* The chickpea patties (keeps for 5 days)

Place in the freezer:
* The courgette and ham loaf, in its tin

14 Prepare the chickpea burgers. In the food processor, place the chickpeas (drained), 1 tablespoon of chopped spring onions, a little chopped garlic, 1 teaspoon of olive oil and 2 tablespoons of cornflour. Process just until the mixture comes together to form a ball. Shape 4 round patties the diameter of the burger buns. Cook the patties for 2 minutes on each side in the frying pan with a little oil. Remove the patties and set them aside.

15 Using a long serrated knife (such as a bread knife), halve the pineapple lengthways. Using a small knife, cut all around the inside edge of the pineapple down through the flesh, being careful not to pierce the skin. Slice the flesh crossways from top and bottom, moving from the outside edge

to the fibrous core. Using a spoon, scoop out the flesh, and discard the fibrous core. Dice the flesh.

16 In the frying pan, heat 1 tablespoon of olive oil until warm. Add half the remaining chopped spring onions, all of the remaining chopped garlic and the remaining peas. Grate the ginger over the top of the mixture. Add 1 tablespoon of soy sauce. Cook for 2 minutes, then add the diced pineapple and the rice, and cook for 5 more minutes.

Menu #4

Monday

Starter
Courgette gazpacho

Main
Tuna and tomato quiche

Reheating time:
10 minutes

Ingredients: the gazpacho, quiche, several lettuce leaves
Serve the gazpacho chilled. Reheat the quiche for
10 minutes in the oven preheated to 180°C/gas mark 4.
Serve with the lettuce leaves on the side.

Cooking and reheating time:
10 minutes
Preparation time:
1 minute

Tuesday

Prawn and pineapple fried rice

Ingredients: olive oil, the frozen prawns, fried rice, pineapple halves, remaining chopped spring onions
In a frying pan or sauté pan, heat 1 tablespoon of olive oil until warm. Heat the prawns for 2 minutes on each side, seasoned with a little salt. Add the fried rice, and reheat it for 5 minutes. Spoon the mixture into the pineapple halves. Sprinkle with the chopped spring onion.
For Wednesday, remove the courgette and ham loaf from the freezer and defrost it in the refrigerator.

Wednesday

Starter
Tzatziki sauce

Main
Courgette and ham loaf

Reheating time:
15 minutes
Preparation time:
5 minutes

Ingredients: two-thirds of the grated cucumbers, the Greek yogurt, remaining chopped mint, remaining garlic clove, juice of half the lemon, the courgette and ham loaf, salt and pepper
Make the tzatziki sauce. In a large serving bowl, combine the grated cucumbers, yogurt, mint, garlic clove (very finely chopped or pressed through a garlic press), lemon juice and salt and pepper. Set aside 4 tablespoons of the tzatziki sauce in a bowl in the refrigerator; this will be used for the sauce on the chickpea burgers for tomorrow. Wrap the remaining lemon half in clingfilm and refrigerate. Reheat the loaf in the oven preheated to 180°C/ gas mark 4. Unmould, and serve.

Thursday

Chickpea burgers

Reheating time:
5 minutes
Preparation time:
10 minutes

Ingredients: the burger buns, chickpea patties, tomato ketchup, remaining tzatziki sauce, 1 tomato, 4 lettuce leaves

Toast the burger buns under the oven broiler or in a toaster. Reheat the chickpea patties in a frying pan. Slice the tomato into rounds. Cut the lettuce leaves into strips. Spread a little ketchup on top of each bottom bun, then place some lettuce strips on top, then a chickpea patty. Spread on 1 tablespoon of tzatziki sauce and top with 1 or 2 slices of tomatoes. Add the top bun, and serve.

Cooking time:
15 minutes
Preparation time:
10 minutes

Friday

Farfalle and smoked salmon salad

Ingredients: the pasta, avocados, remaining tomato, smoked salmon, artichoke hearts, remaining grated cucumber, remaining lettuce, 3 tablespoons of olive oil, the juice of the remaining lemon half, the sweetcorn, salt and pepper

Cook the pasta according to the packet instructions. Meanwhile, dice the avocados, tomato and salmon. Quarter the artichoke hearts. Cut the lettuce leaves into strips. Drain the pasta and rinse it under cold water. In a large bowl, vigorously whisk together the olive oil and lemon juice with a little salt and pepper. Add all the ingredients and stir to combine. Serve.

Autumn

Menu #1

Menu #1

Fruit / Vegetables

* 1 large (1.5–2kg) butternut squash
* 6 carrots
* 1 celery stick
* 1.5kg Charlotte (or waxy) potatoes
* 1 bag lamb's lettuce, sell-by date > 3 days
* 1 large bag pre-washed spinach leaves or baby spinach (about 300g)
* 1 bunch of flat-leaf parsley
* 1 bunch of fresh coriander
* 2 garlic cloves
* 5 onions
* 1 small lemon
* 1 lime
* 1 (3cm) knob of fresh root ginger
* 1 bunch of spring onions
* 1 small cucumber
* 1 small Granny Smith or Golden Delicious apple, or an apple of your choice, preferably organic

Basics

* 2 bay leaves
* Balsamic vinegar
* Olive oil
* Salt, black pepper

Meat / Fish

* 150g smoked lardons (thick-cut cubed bacon) or 2 blocks 200g smoked tofu
* 3 beef cheeks (ask your butcher to cut them into small pieces) or 1.5kg other cuts of beef stew meat (such as chuck)
* 1 pack beef carpaccio (about 200g) sell-by date at least 6 days after purchase

Refrigerator

* 500ml double cream
* 115g grated Parmesan cheese

Store cupboard

* 1 (425g) can chickpeas
* Tahini or sesame oil (optional)
* Ground cumin
* 4 pitta breads
* 100g unsalted cashews
* 250g jasmine rice
* 1 small jar whole chestnuts
* 2 cans (800g) chopped tomatoes
* 100ml red wine
* 2 small fresh red chillies (such as Tabasco) or ¼ tsp chilli powder
* 450g small pasta shells
* 200g rice noodles (rice vermicelli)
* Dried breadcrumbs
* 2 beef stock cubes
* 2 star anise pods
* Fish sauce

Monday

Pasta with beef cheek sauce

Tuesday

Appetizer
Hummus with crudités

Main
Butternut-chestnut soup with lardons
(or smoked tofu)

Wednesday

Appetizer
Lamb's lettuce, green apple and cashew salad

Main
Shepherd's pie

Thursday

Butternut squash and spinach fried rice, toasted cashews

Friday

Vietnamese pho

Steps

Set up

If you have enough work space, set out all the ingredients needed for this cooking session. This includes everything except the lamb's lettuce, lime, apple, lardons, carpaccio, pitta breads, pasta, rice noodles, fish sauce and vinegar. This allows you to have everything at your fingertips and to not lose time searching for the ingredients in the store cupboard or refrigerator.

Set out the necessary equipment:

- 1 lidded flameproof casserole (preferably oven safe)
- 1 large gratin dish (or shallow baking dish)
- 1 large stockpot (or 1 very large saucepan) for cooking the potatoes
- 2 large saucepans
- 1 baking sheet
- 1 sauté pan or 1 large frying pan
- 1 stick blender
- 1 blender or food processor (for puréeing the chickpeas for the hummus)
- 1 salad spinner (or large bowl and clean tea towel)
- 1 food mill (or potato masher)
- 1 large glass container (for storing the raw vegetable sticks)
- 1 (1.5-litre) glass jar (for storing the pho broth)
- 2 small lidded glass jars
- 3 containers: 2 large + 1 medium
- 1 large serving bowl for the hummus
- Kitchen paper (or 1 thin clean and dry tea towel)
- Clingfilm

Everything is now ready for a cooking time of 2 hours.

<u>1</u> Preheat the oven to 180°C/gas mark 4.

<u>2</u> Peel and chop the onions. Set aside one-third of the onions in a container. Peel the carrots. Cut 3 of the carrots into small dice, and cut the other 3 into sticks. Peel the cucumber and cut it into sticks. Refrigerate the vegetable sticks in an airtight container: these will be served for dipping in the hummus. Cut the celery stick into small dice.

<u>3</u> In the casserole, heat 4 tablespoons of olive oil until warm. Add two-thirds of the chopped onions, the diced carrots and the diced celery stick. Season with salt, and cook for 5 minutes over medium heat. Add the pieces of beef cheek and brown them

on all sides. Add the red wine, and cook for a few minutes longer, until the liquid is slightly reduced. Add 1 chopped fresh chilli (or the chilli powder) and the bay leaves; season with salt. Stir to combine, then add the chopped tomatoes. Cover the casserole, then place it in the oven (note: if you are using a dish that is not oven safe, continue cooking on the stovetop). Simmer while you are finishing the remaining cooking, checking from time to time that the meat remains immersed in the liquid.

4 Fill the large stockpot with salted water and bring to a boil. Peel the potatoes and cook them in the large stockpot for about 20 minutes, or just until tender when pierced with a fork.

5 Rinse the rice and cook it in boiling water in a large saucepan until still somewhat firm to the bite.

6 Meanwhile, place the cashews on the baking sheet and toast them for 5 minutes on a rack placed near the top of the oven, stirring halfway through the cooking time. Once cooled, place them in a small jar.

7 Peel the garlic cloves and finely chop them. Set them aside.

8 Drain the rice and leave to cool. Rinse the saucepan, fill it with fresh water, and heat it to make the soup.

9 Peel the butternut squash. Cut it lengthways in half and scrape out the seeds. Cut the flesh into small dice. Set aside a quarter of the diced flesh for the fried rice, and place the rest in the saucepan of boiling water and cook for 20 minutes.

10 Prepare the herbs. Remove any rubber bands from around the stems of the coriander and parsley and immerse the herbs in the salad spinner filled with water (or use a large bowl). Drain the water, then gently spin the herbs dry (or use the clean tea towel); the herbs should be as dry as possible so they stay fresh. Place the herbs in an airtight container between 2 sheets of kitchen paper (or wrapped in the tea towel).

11 Cut off the root ends of the spring onions, strip off the first layer of skin, then thinly slice the onions. Place them in a small glass jar.

12 Drain the potatoes and process them through the food mill (or potato masher). Add 250ml of the cream, half the grated Parmesan, and a little chopped garlic. Stir to thoroughly combine, and set aside.

13 Drain about half the cooking water from the butternut squash, then blend the squash with the stick blender with the remaining cooking water, the remaining cream, the chestnuts and some salt and pepper. Wash the stick blender.

14 Prepare the broth for the pho in the second large saucepan. Peel and slice the ginger. Bring 1.5 litres of water to a boil with the stock cubes, the star anise pods, the ginger and a little piece of chilli. Allow the broth to boil for 5 minutes, remove the chilli, and set the broth aside to cool.

It's all done! Leave to cool.

Place in the refrigerator:
* The casserole with the beef cheek sauce (keeps for 2 days)
* The pan with the butternut-chestnut soup, if you are serving it within 2 days
* The hummus (keeps for 5 days)
* The vegetable sticks (keeps for 5 days)
* The herbs (keeps for 1 week)

Place in the freezer:
* The butternut-chestnut soup, if you are serving it more than 2 days after preparing it
* The pho broth in the glass jar (be sure to leave a little space at the top of the jar)
* The fried rice
* The Shepherd's pie, in its dish, covered with clingfilm
* The chopped spring onions

Store cupboard:
* The toasted cashews

15 In the sauté pan, brown the remaining chopped onions and half the chopped garlic in a little olive oil. Add the remaining cubes of butternut squash. Once the squash pieces begin to brown, add a ladle of the pho broth. Cover, and cook for 10 minutes over low heat. Add the spinach and cook just until wilted. Add the cooked rice and immediately turn off the heat. Leave to cool.

16 Prepare the hummus. In the blender, blend the chickpeas (drained) with the juice of the lemon, 1 tablespoon of tahini (if using), 1 teaspoon of cumin, the remaining chopped garlic, 2 tablespoons of olive oil (or use sesame oil if you do not have tahini) and some salt and pepper. Transfer the mixture to the large serving bowl.

17 Remove the casserole from the oven, remove half the meat and sauce, and transfer them to the baking dish; roughly blend the contents of the baking dish using the stick blender. Place the casserole back in the oven until the cooking session is complete. Spread the mashed potatoes over the meat mixture, and sprinkle the top with the dried breadcrumbs. Place the baking dish on a shelf near the top of the oven, and bake for about 10 minutes (the dish will finish cooking when it's reheated prior to serving).

Menu #1

Menu #1

Monday

Pasta with beef cheek sauce

Reheating time:
15 minutes
Cooking time:
15 minutes
Preparation time:
2 minutes

Ingredients: the beef cheek sauce, pasta shells, remaining grated Parmesan, 4 sprigs of flat-leaf parsley, salt and pepper

Reheat the beef cheek sauce. Meanwhile, cook the pasta according to the packet instructions.

Serve the pasta covered with the beef cheek sauce. Sprinkle the Parmesan on top, then a few leaves of chopped parsley. Season with salt and pepper.

For Tuesday, if you have frozen the butternut-chestnut soup, remove it from the freezer and defrost it in the refrigerator.

Reheating time:
10 minutes
Cooking time:
5 minutes
Preparation time:
5 minutes

Tuesday

Appetizer
Hummus with crudités

Main
Butternut-chestnut soup with lardons
(or smoked tofu)

Ingredients: 2 sprigs of coriander, the hummus, pitta breads, butternut-chestnut soup, lardons (or smoked tofu), carrot and cucumber sticks, salt and pepper

Chop the coriander and sprinkle it over the hummus. Heat the pitta breads in the toaster. Reheat the soup. In a frying pan, brown the lardons (or smoked tofu) in a little olive oil, and divide them among the soup bowls. Serve the vegetable sticks with the hummus and toasted pitta breads as an appetizer and the soup as the main.

For Wednesday, remove the Shepherd's pie from the freezer and defrost it in the refrigerator.

Reheating time:
15 minutes
Preparation time:
5 minutes

Wednesday

Appetizer
Lamb's lettuce, green apple and cashew salad

Main
Shepherd's pie

Ingredients: the apple, 3 tbsp of olive oil, 1 tbsp of balsamic vinegar, the bag of lamb's lettuce, 4 sprigs of parsley or coriander (or a mixture of the two), half the toasted cashews, the Shepherd's pie, salt and pepper
Wash and core the apple and slice it into sticks. In the bottom of a large bowl, vigorously whisk together the oil and vinegar. Season with salt and pepper. Add the lettuce, apple sticks and herbs, and toss to coat. Sprinkle the cashews over the top. Reheat the Shepherd's pie in the oven preheated to 180°C/gas mark 4.
For Thursday, remove the fried rice from the freezer and defrost it in the refrigerator.

Thursday

Butternut squash and spinach fried rice, toasted cashews

Reheating time:
10 minutes
Preparation time:
1 minute

Ingredients: the fried rice, remaining cashews, 4 sprigs coriander
Reheat the fried rice, then sprinkle it with the toasted cashews and chopped coriander.
For Friday, remove the pho broth and the chopped spring onions from the freezer and defrost them in the refrigerator.

Cooking time:
5 minutes
Preparation time:
5 minutes

Friday

Vietnamese pho

Ingredients: the defrosted broth, rice stick noodles, defrosted chopped spring onions, beef carpaccio, lime, 4 tablespoons fish sauce, the remaining coriander
In a saucepan, bring the broth to a boil, then remove it from the heat. Add the noodles and cook for the amount of time indicated on the packet. Meanwhile, slice the carpaccio into thin strips. Place the strips in the broth, add the juice from the lime, the spring onions, the fish sauce and the chopped coriander. Serve.

Menu #2

Menu #2

Menu #2

Fruit / Vegetables

* 3 medium sweet potatoes
* 1kg Charlotte (or waxy) potatoes
* 1 large head of cauliflower
* 1 small bag rocket (about 140g), sell-by date > 4 or 5 days after purchase
* about 250g shredded cabbage, sell-by date > 4 or 5 days
* 1 small container cherry tomatoes (about 170g)
* 1 bunch of flat-leaf parsley
* 1 bunch of chives
* 8 garlic cloves
* 2 onions
* 1 small organic lemon
* 1 (5cm) knob of fresh root ginger
* 500g small button mushrooms

Meat / Fish

* About 12 cooked, peeled prawns (sell-by date > 1 or 2 days)
* 400g boneless, skinless chicken breasts
* 4 slices ham (or turkey breast)
* 400g cod loin (fresh or frozen)

Refrigerator

* 500ml double cream
* 450g crème fraîche
* 1 litre whole milk
* 6 large eggs
* 1 small container fresh mini mozzarella cheese balls (about 125g drained)
* 30g unsalted butter
* 115g grated Parmesan cheese
* 115g Parmesan cheese shavings or 115g Parmesan cheese to make shavings

Basics

* Curry powder
* Whole nutmeg
* Herbes de Provence
* Mustard
* Olive oil
* Salt, black pepper

Store cupboard

* 200g basmati or brown rice
* 450g linguine (or spaghetti)
* 250 g instant polenta
* 1 (400g) can chopped tomatoes
* 1 small jar passata (about 280g)
* 400–500ml coconut milk
* 50g walnut halves

Monday

Appetizer
Cauliflower velouté
with sautéed prawns

Main
Polenta pizza with
mushrooms

Tuesday

Sweet potato*** and
chicken curry

Wednesday

Cauliflower and potato
gratin with ham*

Thursday

Appetizer
Cabbage, egg and
cherry tomato salad
with creamy dressing

Main
Linguine** with garlic
cream, rocket, walnuts
and Parmesan

Friday

Cod and sweet potato
fish pie***

*For a pork-free menu, replace the ham with turkey breast.
**For a gluten-free menu, choose gluten-free pasta.
***If you do not like sweet potatoes, replace half the quantity with carrots (for the curry)
and the other half with regular potatoes (for the fish pie), and follow the instructions
exactly as written.

Steps

Set up

If you have enough work space, set out all the ingredients needed for this cooking session. This includes everything except the rocket, shredded cabbage, cherry tomatoes, prawns, Parmesan shavings, rice and pasta. This allows you to have everything at your fingertips and to not lose time searching for the ingredients in the store cupboard or refrigerator.

Set out the necessary equipment:

* 2 small gratin dishes (or shallow baking dishes)
* 1 frying pan
* 1 large stockpot (or very large saucepan)
* 1 large steam cooker or lidded saucepan with a steam basket
* 1 small bowl
* 1 large mixing bowl
* 1 baking sheet
* 1 small saucepan
* 1 sauté pan
* 1 small grater or zester (for the lemon zest and nutmeg)
* 1 stick blender
* 1 salad spinner (or large bowl and a clean tea towel)
* 1 food mill (or potato masher)
* 2 (1.5-litre) glass jars (for the garlic cream and the velouté)
* 1 small lidded jar
* 5 containers: 2 large + 3 small
* Kitchen paper (or a clean tea towel)
* Baking paper, clingfilm, aluminium foil

Everything is now ready for a cooking time of 2 hours 10 minutes.

1 Fill the stockpot with salted water and bring it to a simmer. Wash the cauliflower and cut it into florets. Place the florets in the simmering water, and cook for 15 minutes.

2 Peel the sweet potatoes and the Charlotte potatoes. Cut the sweet potatoes into large dice, and slice the Charlotte potatoes into thin rounds. Place the potato cubes and rounds together in the steam cooker, with the cubes on the bottom and the rounds on top. Cook for about 15 minutes; they should remain somewhat firm.

3 Preheat the oven to 220°C/gas mark 7. Drain the cauliflower. Remove half the cauliflower, and

154

blend it with the stick blender with 200ml of the cream. Add a little water (about 200ml) to obtain a smooth, creamy consistency. Season with salt and pepper. Transfer the mixture to a jar. Roughly blend the remaining cauliflower and combine it with 3 tablespoons of crème fraîche, a little freshly grated nutmeg and salt and pepper. Cut the ham slices into squares and stir to combine them into the mixture.

4 At this point, the potato rounds should be cooked. Remove half of them, and place them in the bottom of a baking dish. Pour the cauliflower-ham mixture over the top of the potatoes. Top with a quarter of the grated Parmesan and bake for 20 minutes, or until browned and bubbling. Rinse and dry the stockpot.

5 Place the cod in a separate baking dish. Season with salt, and pre-cook it for 3 minutes (5 minutes if frozen) in the microwave (or in the oven for double the amount of time).

6 Meanwhile, wash the chives and parsley by immersing them in a large volume of cold water, then gently dry them in the clean tea towel or in the salad spinner. Chop three-quarters of the chives and place them in the small bowl. Place the parsley and remaining chives in an airtight container between 2 sheets of kitchen paper.

7 Drain the cooking liquid from the cod, and flake the cod into the bottom of the baking dish. Add 3 tablespoons of crème fraîche, the chopped chives, a little grated zest from the lemon, and season with a little pepper. Stir to combine.

8 Place the eggs in the small saucepan filled with water and cook them for 8 minutes after the water begins to boil.

9 Using the food mill (or potato masher), in the large mixing bowl, mash the remaining cooked potato rounds with half the cooked sweet potatoes. Add the remaining crème fraîche, season with salt and pepper, and stir to combine. Spread this mixture on top of the cod. Bake for 15 minutes, or just until the cod is cooked through.

10 At this point, the eggs should be cooked. Rinse them under cold water to stop the cooking, and refrigerate them for up to 5 days.

11 Prepare the polenta. In the stockpot, place the whole milk and ½ teaspoon of salt. Bring the milk to a simmer, and sprinkle the polenta into the pan. Reduce the heat, and cook for 1 minute while whisking constantly. Add the butter and the remaining grated Parmesan. Stir to combine, and cool slightly.

12 Meanwhile, peel and chop the garlic cloves and the onions. Cut off and discard the mushroom stems, and gently wash and dry the tops. Cut the tops in half or into quarters, depending on their size.

13 In the frying pan, heat 2 tablespoons of olive oil, and add the equivalent of 2 chopped garlic cloves, the mushrooms and ½ teaspoon of salt. Cook for 5 minutes over medium heat, just until the mushrooms are no longer releasing any liquid. At the end of the cooking time, chop half the parsley and sprinkle it over the mushrooms.

It's all done! Leave to cool.

Place in the refrigerator:
* The cauliflower velouté in the large jar, leaving a little air at the top (keeps for 2 days)
* The polenta pizza, preferably on the baking sheet, covered with foil (keeps for 2 days)
* The sweet potato and chicken curry (keeps for 2 days)
* The hard-boiled eggs (keeps for 5 days)
* The creamy dressing
* The remaining parsley and chives
* The chopped garlic and ginger mixture

Place in the freezer:
* The sweet potato and chicken curry, if you are serving it more than 2 days after preparing it
* The cauliflower and potato gratin, in its baking dish, covered with clingfilm
* The garlic cream
* The cod and sweet potato fish pie, in its baking dish, covered with clingfilm

Store cupboard:
* The toasted walnuts

14 Meanwhile, line a baking sheet with baking paper and spread the cooled polenta out into a 1.5cm-thick oval. Spread the passata over the top of the polenta, leaving a 2cm border, then distribute the mozzarella balls and the cooked parsley and mushrooms over the top. Sprinkle on 1 tablespoon of the herbes de Provence. Bake for 5 minutes, or until the cheese is melted.

15 In the sauté pan, heat 2 tablespoons of olive oil until warm. Add a quarter of the remaining chopped garlic, the chopped onions, some salt and 1 tablespoon of curry powder. Cook for 5 minutes, or until browned. Peel and chop the ginger. Add three-quarters of the ginger to the pan. Place the remaining ginger and one-quarter of the remaining garlic in an airtight container and refrigerate. Cut the chicken breasts into cubes and brown them in the

pan. Add the chopped tomatoes and the coconut milk. Simmer for 15 minutes.

16 Meanwhile, toast the walnuts in the warm oven (turned off) for 5 minutes. In the frying pan, heat 2 tablespoons of olive oil until warm, and cook the remaining chopped garlic with ½ teaspoon of salt. Cook for 2 minutes, or until lightly browned, then add 200ml of the cream. Cook for 2 minutes then transfer the mixture to the jar. Place the walnuts in the small jar.

17 Prepare the creamy dressing for the cabbage salad. In a small container, vigorously whisk together 1 teaspoon of mustard, ½ teaspoon of salt and the juice and remaining zest of the lemon while adding the remaining cream a little at a time, until smooth. Add the remaining sweet potatoes to the chicken curry.

Menu #2

Menu #2

Monday

Appetizer
Cauliflower velouté with sautéed prawns

Main
Polenta pizza with mushrooms

Reheating time:
10 minutes
Cooking time:
2 minutes
Preparation time:
2 minutes

Ingredients: the polenta pizza, cauliflower velouté, 1 tbsp olive oil, the garlic-ginger mixture, 3 sprigs of parsley, the peeled prawns, salt and pepper

Reheat the polenta pizza in the oven preheated to 160°C/gas mark 3. Reheat the cauliflower velouté in a saucepan while stirring. In a small frying pan, heat the olive oil. Add the chopped garlic and ginger. Chop the parsley and sprinkle it over the prawns. Add the prawns to the pan and cook for 1–2 minutes. Top each bowl of velouté with some of this mixture and serve.

For Tuesday, if the sweet potato and chicken curry is frozen, remove it from the freezer and defrost it in the refrigerator.

Reheating time:
15 minutes
Cooking time:
10 minutes
Preparation time:
3 minutes

Tuesday

Sweet potato and chicken curry

Ingredients: the sweet potato and chicken curry, rice, remaining chives, salt and pepper

Reheat the curry. Thoroughly rinse the rice and cook it according to the packet instructions. Serve it on the side with a sprinkle of chives.

For Wednesday, remove the cauliflower and potato gratin from the freezer and defrost it in the refrigerator.

Reheating time:
15 minutes

Wednesday

Cauliflower and potato gratin with ham

Ingredients: the cauliflower and potato gratin
Reheat the gratin in the oven preheated to 150°C/gas mark 2, and serve.
For Thursday, remove the garlic cream from the freezer and defrost it in the refrigerator.

Thursday

Reheating time:
5 minutes
Cooking time:
15 minutes
Preparation time:
10 minutes

Appetizer
Cabbage, egg and cherry tomato salad with creamy dressing

Main
Linguine with garlic cream, rocket, walnuts and Parmesan

Ingredients: the linguine, defrosted garlic cream, hard-boiled eggs, cherry tomatoes, shredded cabbage, remaining parsley, the creamy dressing, bag of rocket, the toasted walnuts, Parmesan shavings, olive oil, salt and pepper
Cook the pasta according to the packet instructions.
Reheat the garlic cream.
Meanwhile, peel the hard-boiled eggs and cut them into quarters. Cut the cherry tomatoes into quarters. Place the shredded cabbage in a large shallow serving dish, top with the cherry tomatoes and hard-boiled eggs. Sprinkle with the chopped parsley. Pour the creamy dressing over the top. Serve the pasta with the garlic cream, topped with the rocket, walnuts and Parmesan shavings. Season with pepper and a drizzle of olive oil.
For Friday, remove the fish pie from the freezer and defrost it in the refrigerator.

Reheating time:
15 minutes

Friday

Cod and sweet potato fish pie

Ingredients: the fish pie
Reheat the fish pie in the oven preheated to 160°C/gas mark 3, and serve.

Menu #3

Menu #3

Menu #3

Fruit / Vegetables

* 1 head of chicory
* 6 Charlotte (or other waxy) potatoes (170g)
* 1kg frozen chopped spinach
* 2 small quinces
* 1.2kg turnips
* 4 carrots
* 2 leeks
* 1 bunch of fresh coriander
* 1 bunch of chives
* 5 garlic cloves
* 5 onions
* 2 red onions
* 1 small organic lemon

Meat / Fish

* 1kg boneless lamb shoulder, cut into small pieces by your butcher
* 2 fresh skinless salmon fillets
* 4 slices smoked salmon
* 150g lardons*, or 200g smoked tofu

Refrigerator

* 1 litre whole milk
* 300g fromage frais
* 120–180g fresh goats' cheese
* 1 sheet of ready-rolled shortcrust pastry
* 250g fresh lasagne
* 125g unsalted butter
* 500ml double cream

Basics

* 80g plain flour
* Potato starch or cornflour
* Whole nutmeg
* Olive oil
* Salt, black pepper

Store cupboard

* 1 (142g) can tuna
* 1 (425g) can chickpeas
* 200g couscous
* 6 tbsp honey
* Ground cumin
* Ground cinnamon
* Ras el hanout

Monday

Appetizer
Tuna rillettes chicory bites

Main
Turnip, honey and goats' cheese tart Tatin

Tuesday

Lamb tagine with quince

Wednesday

Appetizer
Spinach velouté

Main
Potato, leek, onion and bacon* gratin

Thursday

Lamb koftas, pan-fried carrots, turnips and chickpeas with cumin

Friday

Salmon and spinach lasagne

*For a pork-free menu, replace the lardons with smoked tofu.

Set up

If you have enough work space, set out all the ingredients needed for this cooking session. This includes everything except the chicory and the couscous. This allows you to have everything at your fingertips and to not lose time searching for the ingredients in the store cupboard or refrigerator.

Set out the necessary equipment:

* 3 small bowls
* 2 large baking dishes
* 1 large sauté pan
* 1 large saucepan
* 1 medium saucepan
* 1 lidded cast-iron casserole or stockpot
* 1 20cm flan tin
* 1 small grater or zester (for the lemon zest and nutmeg)
* 1 food processor (for grinding the lamb meat for the meatballs)
* 1 stick blender
* 1 large microwave-safe bowl
* 1 large bowl (for the tuna rillettes)
* 1 1.5-litre glass jar (for storing the velouté)
* 2 containers: 1 large + 1 small
* Baking paper, clingfilm, aluminium foil, kitchen paper, airtight storage bag

Everything is now ready for a cooking time of 2 hours.

1 Peel and roughly chop both types of onions and the garlic cloves. Set aside in separate bowls.

2 In the casserole, melt 20 g of the butter with 1 tablespoon of olive oil. Add half the chopped onions, half the garlic cloves, ½ teaspoon of cumin, ½ teaspoon of cinnamon and 1 teaspoon of salt. Cook for 2 minutes, or until slightly softened. Add the lamb and 3 tablespoons of honey, stir, then add just over 200 ml of water. Bring to the boil, then reduce the heat and simmer, covered, for 1 hour.

3 Meanwhile, peel the potatoes, turnips, carrots and quinces. Thoroughly wash the leeks (including in between the leaves) and thinly slice. Cut 3 of the potatoes into rounds and 3 of them into large dice.

4 In the large sauté pan, heat 2 tablespoons of olive oil, then add the remaining chopped onions, the sliced leeks, the potato rounds and 1 teaspoon of salt. Cook for 30 minutes, covered, stirring from time to time.

5 Prepare a béchamel sauce (it will be used for two of the recipes. In the large saucepan, gently melt 80g of the butter, then add the flour. Stir with a wooden spoon, just until all of the butter is absorbed into the flour and the mixture forms a sort of paste. Pour in all of the milk at once. Cook over medium heat while stirring constantly, just until the mixture thickens (about 10 minutes). Off the heat, season with 1 teaspoon of salt, a little pepper and a little grated nutmeg. Transfer the béchamel sauce to the large container.

6 Preheat the oven to 180°C/gas mark 4. Wash the large saucepan, half fill with salted water, and bring it to a boil. Meanwhile, cut the quinces into quarters. Remove and discard the fibrous core and the seeds, as if coring an apple.

7 As soon as the water begins to boil, add the whole turnips and cook for 15 minutes. Chop the quinces into large pieces and set aside.

8 Transfer the pan-fried mixture of leeks, onion, and potatoes to a large baking dish. In the same sauté pan (do not rinse it), brown the lardons (or the smoked diced tofu) for 2 minutes over high heat. Add the lardons to the baking dish. Add the cream, and stir to thoroughly combine all the ingredients. Spread one-third of the béchamel sauce over the top. Bake for 30 minutes, or until golden on top and bubbling.

9 Drain the turnips and rinse them under cold water. Cut them into quarters. Add the quince pieces to the pan containing the lamb, and cook for 20 minutes.

10 Wash the large saucepan. Melt the remaining 25 g of the butter with 1 tablespoon of olive oil. Add the remaining honey and three-quarters of the turnips. Cook for 15 minutes, covered, turning them once halfway through the cooking time. Cook for 10 more minutes, uncovered, just until the liquid evaporates and the turnips are well caramelized.

11 While the turnips are cooking, place the chopped spinach in the microwave-safe bowl, and microwave it on low to defrost. Meanwhile, bring 350ml of salted water to a boil in the medium saucepan. Add the diced potatoes and cook for 10 minutes. Add one-third of the thawed spinach and cook for 5 minutes. Season the remaining chopped spinach with salt. Zest and juice the lemon, and set the zest and juice aside.

12 Line the bottom of the flan tin with a circle of baking paper cut to the same diameter as the tin. Arrange the cooked turnips in the bottom of the tin, overlapping them closely together, then crumble the goats' cheese over the top. Drape the pastry over the turnips, folding the edge down and inside the tin to form an attractive border. Prick the pastry several times with the tip of a knife to allow steam to escape. Bake for 25 minutes, or until golden on top.

13 In the bottom of the separate large baking dish, spread a layer of the béchamel sauce. Cut up the salmon fillets into bite-size pieces. Cover the sauce with a layer of the lasagne, then cover with one-third of the remaining spinach.

It's all done! Leave to cool.

Place in the refrigerator:

* The tuna rillettes
* The tart Tatin, in its tin, covered with foil
* The lamb tagine, in its pan (keeps for 2 days)
* The remaining coriander, rolled up in kitchen paper and placed in an airtight storage bag

Place in the freezer:

* The lamb tagine, if you are serving it more than 2 days after preparing it
* The spinach velouté, in the large jar, leaving a little air at the top
* The leek and potato gratin, in its baking dish, covered with clingfilm
* The lamb koftas with the cooked turnip-carrot-chickpea mixture, in a large airtight container
* The salmon and spinach lasagne, directly in the baking dish covered with clingfilm

Top with pieces of salmon, then a torn slice of the smoked salmon, some lemon juice and a little more béchamel sauce. Repeat until all of the ingredients are used. Bake for 30 minutes, or until golden on top, on a shelf set below the tart Tatin.

__14__ In the same pan used to cook the turnips (do not wash the pan), heat 2 tablespoons of olive oil, then add half the chopped red onions. Season with a little salt, and cook until lightly browned. Meanwhile, cut the carrots into rounds. Add them to the pan with the remaining turnips and ½ teaspoon of cumin. Cook for 20 minutes. At the end of the cooking time, add the chickpeas (drained) and stir.

__15__ To the saucepan with the spinach and potatoes, add two-thirds of the fromage frais and 2 small pieces of chopped garlic. Using the stick blender, blend for several minutes until smooth.

__16__ Remove the lamb, quince, and onions from the pan. Bring the cooking juices to the boil and reduce slightly. Meanwhile, prepare the lamb koftas. Place half the lamb in the food processor with the remaining chopped garlic and red onions, a quarter of the coriander, 1 teaspoon of salt, a little pepper, ½ teaspoon of ras el hanout and 1 tablespoon of potato starch. Pulse to combine, then shape the mixture into balls using your hands. In the sauté pan, heat a little oil, then cook the meatballs for 10 minutes, stirring frequently. Return the remaining lamb and quince to the pan. Add some chopped coriander.

__17__ Make the tuna rillettes by combining the remaining fromage frais in the large bowl with the tuna (drained), chopped chives and the lemon zest.

Menu #3

Monday

Appetizer
**Tuna rillettes
chicory bites**

Main
**Turnip, honey and
goats' cheese
tart Tatin**

Reheating time:
10 minutes
Preparation time:
2 minutes

Ingredients: the tuna rillettes, chicory, tart Tatin
Pull off the individual leaves of the chicory and fill each
one with a little of the tuna rillettes.
Reheat the tart Tatin in the oven preheated to 160°C/
gas mark 3.
**For Tuesday, if you have frozen the lamb tagine, remove
it from the freezer and defrost it in the refrigerator.**

Reheating time:
15 minutes
Cooking time:
5 minutes
Preparation time:
1 minute

Tuesday

**Lamb tagine with
quince**

Ingredients: the lamb tagine, couscous, half the remaining
coriander
Reheat the lamb tagine in its pot. Cook the couscous
according to the packet instructions.
Serve the couscous on plates, topped with the lamb tagine,
and sprinkled with chopped coriander.
**For Wednesday, remove the spinach velouté and the
potato and leek gratin from the freezer and defrost
them in the refrigerator.**

Reheating time:
15 minutes

Wednesday

Appetizer
Spinach and fromage frais velouté

Main
Potato, leek, onion, and bacon gratin

Ingredients: the potato and leek gratin, the spinach velouté
Reheat the gratin in the oven preheated to 160°C/gas mark 3. Reheat the velouté in a saucepan, and serve.
For Thursday, remove the lamb koftas and the turnip-carrot-chickpea mixture from the freezer and defrost them in the refrigerator.

Thursday

Lamb koftas, panfried carrots, turnips and chickpeas with cumin

Reheating time:
15 minutes

Ingredients: the koftas, turnip-carrot-chickpea mixture, remaining coriander
Reheat the koftas in a sauté pan. Sprinkle them with chopped coriander. Warm the vegetable mixture in the same pan and serve it with the koftas.
For Friday, remove the salmon and spinach lasagne from the freezer and defrost it in the refrigerator.

Reheating time:
15 minutes

Friday

Salmon and spinach lasagne

Ingredients: the salmon and spinach lasagne
Reheat the lasagne in the oven preheated to 160°C/gas mark 3, and serve.

Menu #4

Menu #4

Fruit / Vegetables

* 1 (2kg) fresh pumpkin
* 800g small potatoes
* 1 head of broccoli
* 2 carrots
* 1 small container cherry tomatoes (about 170g)
* 1 celery stick
* 1 bunch of fresh coriander
* 6 garlic cloves
* 6 onions
* 6 shallots

Basics

* Plain flour
* Wine vinegar
* Olive oil
* Salt, black pepper

Meat / Fish

* 3 skin-on chicken legs
* 4 frozen pollack fillets (or other white fish)
* 4 slices ham* (or turkey)

Refrigerator

* 100g grated Parmesan cheese
* 375g crème fraîche
* 70–100g grated Gruyère cheese
* 125g unsalted butter
* 330ml double cream
* 1 sheet of ready-rolled puff pastry (about 227g)

Store cupboard

* 250g macaroni
* 250g white or brown rice
* 1 (400g) can red kidney beans, drained
* 1 (400g) can tomatoes, in their juice
* 200g couscous
* Ground cinnamon
* Ground turmeric
* Ground cumin
* Curry powder
* Ground ginger
* Dried thyme
* 1 handful dried pumpkin seeds

Monday

Appetizer
Cherry tomatoes, Parmesan, pumpkin seeds and thyme in flaky pastry

Main
Vegetarian chilli

Tuesday

Pumpkin and chicken couscous

Wednesday

Ham* and broccoli pasta bake

Thursday

Chicken and vegetable crumble

Friday

Appetizer
Curried pumpkin soup

Main
Pollack in a shallot sauce with steamed potatoes

*For a pork-free menu, replace the ham with sliced turkey breast.

Set up

If you have enough work space, set out all the ingredients needed for this cooking session. This includes everything except the potatoes, pollack, puff pastry sheet, rice and couscous. This allows you to have everything at your fingertips and to not lose time searching for the ingredients in the store cupboard or refrigerator.

Set out the necessary equipment:

* 1 baking sheet
* 2 gratin dishes (or shallow baking dishes)
* 1 large sauté pan
* 1 large saucepan
* 1 small saucepan
* 1 lidded cast-iron casserole or stockpot
* 1 stick blender
* 1 skimmer (or slotted spoon)
* 1 large mixing bowl
* 1 small mixing bowl
* 3 small bowls
* 1 (1.5-litre) glass jar (for storing the soup)
* 1 salad spinner (or large bowl and clean tea towel)
* 2 containers: 1 large + 1 small
* Kitchen paper, aluminium foil, clingfilm, baking paper

Everything is now ready for a cooking time of 1 hour 50 minutes.

1 In the large sauté pan, heat 2 tablespoons of olive oil until warm. Add the chicken legs skin side down. Cover, and cook for 10 minutes, or until browned.

2 Peel and roughly chop the onions, shallots and garlic cloves. Place them separately in the small bowls.

3 Fill the salad spinner (or a large bowl) with water and soak the coriander for 5 minutes. Drain, then gently spin the coriander dry (or use the tea towel). Place the coriander in a glass container between 2 sheets of kitchen paper. Refrigerate for up to 1 week.

4 Turn off the heat under the chicken. Peel the carrots and wash the celery stick. Cut the carrots and celery into small dice. Turn the chicken legs over (be careful of spattering), add a quarter of the onions and garlic and all of the carrots and celery. Season with salt, add ½ teaspoon of cinnamon and ½ teaspoon of ground ginger. Turn on the heat under the chicken to low. Add about 190ml water, cover, and cook for 35 minutes.

5 Prepare the vegetarian chilli: In the cast-iron casserole, heat 2 tablespoons of olive oil until warm, then add one-third of the remaining onions and garlic and 1 teaspoon of salt. Cook for 10 minutes, covered, over low heat.

6 Meanwhile, cut the pumpkin in half, scrape out and discard the seeds, then peel the flesh and cut it into large cubes. Add 1 handful of the cubes to

a gratin dish that will be used with the crumble topping. Place the remaining cubes in the large mixing bowl.

7 To the casserole, add the canned tomatoes with their juice, ½ teaspoon of turmeric, and ½ teaspoon of cumin. Continue cooking for another 15 minutes.

8 Fill the large saucepan with salted water and bring it to a boil. Meanwhile, wash the broccoli and cut it into very small florets. Add the florets to the saucepan, stir to incorporate, then cook for 10 minutes.

9 Preheat the oven to 180°C/gas mark 4. Prepare the crumble topping in the small mixing bowl by combining 150g flour, the butter, 60g of the Parmesan, 1 pinch of thyme and half the dried pumpkin seeds. Set aside.

183

10 Remove the cooked broccoli florets from the saucepan using the skimmer, and transfer them to a bowl. Add the macaroni to the pan. Cook just until the pasta is al dente (still firm to the bite).

11 Drain and rinse the beans and add them to the casserole. Stir to combine, and turn off the heat.

Remove 1 chicken leg from the sauté pan and set it aside on a plate to cool. Cut the cherry tomatoes in half. Place half of them in the gratin dish with the pumpkin cubes. Add one-third of the broccoli florets, half the remaining onions and garlic and a little salt. Shred the flesh of the chicken leg that is cooling on the plate. Add the shredded meat to the gratin dish, and stir to combine. Cover the mixture with the crumble topping. Bake for 30 minutes, or until golden on top.

12 To the small saucepan, add 50ml vinegar and all of the shallots. Cook over low heat for about 15 minutes, just until almost all of the vinegar has evaporated.

13 Drain the pasta and place it in the separate gratin dish. Add the remaining broccoli, the cream and half the remaining garlic to the dish. Dice the ham, add it to the gratin dish, season with salt and pepper, and stir to thoroughly combine. Sprinkle the grated Gruyère over the top and bake for 15 minutes, or until the cheese is melted and golden. Wash the large saucepan, fill it half full with water, and bring it to a boil.

184

It's all done! Leave to cool.

Place in the refrigerator:
* The puff pastry squares, directly on the baking sheet, covered in foil (keeps for 2 days)
* The vegetarian chilli, in the pan (keeps for 3 days)
* The pumpkin and chicken (keeps for 2 days)
* The coriander, in its airtight container (keeps for 1 week)

Place in the freezer:
* The pumpkin and chicken, if you are serving it more than 2 days after preparing it
* The soup, in the large jar, leaving a little room at the top
* The ham and broccoli pasta bake, in its gratin dish, covered with clingfilm
* The chicken and vegetable crumble, in its gratin dish, covered with clingfilm
* The shallot sauce, in an airtight container

14 To the sauté pan with the chicken legs, add one-third of the pumpkin cubes. Continue cooking for 10 more minutes, or until the chicken is cooked through and the vegetables are softened.

15 To the saucepan of boiling water, add the remaining pumpkin cubes, garlic and onions. Cook for 15 minutes.

16 To the small saucepan with the shallots, add two-thirds of the crème fraîche (about 250g), and season with salt and pepper. Set aside off the heat.

17 Remove the puff pastry sheet from the refrigerator, roll it out, and cut it into 12 x 10cm squares. Place 3 cherry tomato halves in the centre of each puff pastry square, and gather the ends to the centre and pinch them together to seal.

Sprinkle the squares with the remaining Parmesan, some thyme and some pumpkin seeds. Place the squares on the baking sheet lined with baking paper and bake for 10 minutes, or until puffed and golden.

18 To the large saucepan with the pumpkin, add the remaining crème fraîche and ½ teaspoon of curry powder. Blend thoroughly with the stick blender.

Menu #4

Monday

Appetizer
Cherry tomatoes, Parmesan, pumpkin seeds and thyme in flaky pastry

Main
Vegetarian chilli

Reheating time:
10 minutes
Cooking time:
10 minutes
Preparation time:
1 minute

Ingredients: the rice, puff pastry squares, vegetarian chilli, half the coriander
Cook the rice according to the packet instructions. Reheat the puff pastry squares in the oven preheated to 160°C/ gas mark 3. Reheat the chilli in its pan. Serve with the rice, sprinkled with coriander.
For Tuesday, if you have frozen the pumpkin and chicken, remove it from the freezer and defrost it in the refrigerator.

Reheating time:
15 minutes
Cooking time:
5 minutes
Preparation time:
1 minute

Tuesday

Pumpkin and chicken couscous

Ingredients: the pumpkin and chicken, couscous, the remaining coriander
Reheat the pumpkin and chicken in a sauté pan. Cook the couscous according to the packet instructions. Serve the couscous on plates, with the pumpkin and chicken ladled over the top and sprinkled with chopped coriander.
For Wednesday, remove the ham and broccoli pasta bake from the freezer and defrost it in the refrigerator

Wednesday

Ham and broccoli pasta bake

Reheating time:
15 minutes

Ingredients: the ham and broccoli pasta bake
Reheat the pasta bake in the oven preheated to 160°C/ gas mark 3, and serve.
For Thursday, remove the crumble from the freezer and defrost it in the refrigerator.

Thursday

Reheating time:
15 minutes

Chicken and vegetable crumble

Ingredients: the chicken and vegetable crumble
Reheat the crumble in the oven preheated to 160°C/ gas mark 3, and serve.
For Friday, remove the pumpkin soup and the shallot sauce from the freezer and defrost them in the refrigerator.

Reheating time:
15 minutes
Cooking time:
15 minutes
Preparation time:
2 minutes

Friday

Appetizer
Curried pumpkin soup

Main
Pollack in a shallot sauce with steamed potatoes

Ingredients: the potatoes, frozen pollack fillets, pumpkin soup, shallot sauce
Steam the whole potatoes, skin on, for 15 minutes, or until tender when pierced with a fork. Cook the fish according to the packet instructions (or according to your preference). Meanwhile, reheat the soup in a large saucepan, and the shallot sauce in a small saucepan. Serve the pollack and the potatoes with the sauce spooned over the top.

Winter

Menu #1

Menu #1

Shopping list

Menu #1

Fruit / Vegetables

* 6 leeks
* 8 carrots
* 1 celery stick
* 4 turnips
* 2kg Charlotte (or waxy) potatoes
* 1 bunch of flat-leaf parsley
* 2 onions
* 1 garlic clove

Basics

* 3 bay leaves
* 3 large peppercorns
* Dried thyme
* Mustard
* Vinegar
* Sunflower oil
* Olive oil
* Salt, fleur de sel sea salt, coarse sea salt, black pepper

Meat / Fish

* 1.5kg stewing beef (a mixture of rib, chuck, and shin)
* 1–4 marrowbones, according to your tastes
* 400g smoked haddock fillets

Refrigerator

* 6 large eggs
* 400ml double cream

Store cupboard

* 200ml coconut milk
* 1 small jar cornichons (gherkins), about 200g
* 200g orzo pasta (or broken vermicelli)
* 4 slices rustic bread
* 1 pack filo pastry
* 3 whole cloves

Monday

Appetizer
Leeks in vinaigrette
with devilled eggs

Main
Orzo pasta in beef
broth

Tuesday

Pot-au-feu

Wednesday

Appetizer
Beef and vegetable
samosas

Main
Haddock brandade

Thursday

Vegetable velouté,
marrow toasts

Friday

Haddock and coconut
milk soup

Steps

Set up

If you have enough work space, set out all the ingredients needed for this cooking session. This includes everything except 1 egg, the pasta, cornichons, mustard, sunflower oil and fleur de sel sea salt. This allows you to have everything at your fingertips and to not lose time searching for the ingredients in the store cupboard or refrigerator.

Set out the necessary equipment:
* 1 small saucepan
* 1 medium saucepan
* 1 very large saucepan
* 1 large lidded cast-iron casserole or 1 stockpot (for making the pot-au-feu)
* 2 large mixing bowls
* 1 gratin dish (or shallow baking dish)
* 1 food mill (or potato masher)
* 1 stick blender
* 1 skimmer (or slotted spoon)
* 1 colander
* 2 (1.5-litre) glass jars (for storing the pot-au-feu broth and the velouté)
* 6 containers: 3 large + 2 medium + 1 small
* Clingfilm

Everything is now ready for a cooking time of 2 hours.

1 Place the pieces of beef (but not the marrowbones) in the cast-iron casserole. Add 3 litres of water, 1 tablespoon of coarse sea salt, 2 bay leaves and 1 onion that has been peeled and studded with the cloves. Bring to a boil. Cook, uncovered, for 15 minutes, skimming the fat from the surface during that time, then lower the heat.

2 Meanwhile, in the medium saucepan, heat the coconut milk with 500ml water, 1 bay leaf and ½ teaspoon of dried thyme.

3 Thoroughly rinse the haddock fillets under cold water to remove excess salt. Remove the skin using your fingers. Cut the fillets into pieces, then place

them in the saucepan in the coconut milk. Cook over very low heat for 15 minutes without boiling.

4 Fill the very large saucepan with salted water and bring it to a boil. Peel all the potatoes. Cook the potatoes whole in the saucepan just until tender when pierced with a fork (about 30 minutes).

5 Remove the pieces of haddock from the saucepan using the skimmer, and place them in the colander set over a plate to drain (do not drain the saucepan).

6 Peel the turnips, carrots, and the remaining onion. Dice 1 turnip and cut the remaining turnips in half. Cut 2 of the carrots into rounds and cut the remaining carrots into quarters. Dice the onion.

7 To the saucepan used to poach the haddock, add the diced turnips and onion and the carrot rounds. Cook for 30 minutes, covered; do not add salt during this time.

8 To the pan with the beef, add the turnip halves, carrot pieces, peppercorns and 1 sprig of parsley.

9 Cut off the root ends of the leeks, thoroughly wash the leeks (including in between the leaves), and cut them each into 4 sections. Pick the leaves off the celery stick, wash it and cut it into 4 equal pieces. Add the celery and leeks to the pan with the beef.

Steps

10 In the large mixing bowl, flake half the pieces of haddock. Peel and chop the garlic clove and add it to the bowl, then add 200ml of the cream, 2 tablespoons of olive oil, and two-thirds of the cooked potatoes. Season with pepper but do not add salt. Process the mixture using the food mill (or potato masher).

11 Wash and dry the parsley, then finely chop it. Add half the chopped parsley to the haddock mixture. Stir to combine, then transfer it to the gratin dish. Wash out the bowl.

12 Place the remaining haddock fillets in the saucepan with the vegetables and coconut milk. Turn off the heat and leave to cool.

13 Add water to the small saucepan and bring it to a boil. Cook 4 of the eggs in the boiling water for 10 minutes.

14 Remove all of the vegetables from the pan with the beef using the skimmer. Set aside 8 attractive sections of the leeks in a small container to serve with the leek vinaigrette. Sprinkle them with 1 tablespoon of chopped parsley. Set aside the most attractive pieces of carrots, turnips, leeks, celery and onion to serve on the side with the pot-au-feu.

15 Remove half the meat from the ribs and shred it. Combine the shredded meat with 3 of the potatoes, 2 pieces of turnip, several carrot rounds, the remaining chopped parsley and salt and pepper.

It's all done! Leave to cool.

Place in the refrigerator:
* The 4 hard-boiled eggs (keeps for 5 days)
* The 8 sections of cooked leeks (keeps for 3 days)
* The pot-au-feu broth, in the glass jar (keeps for 3 days)
* The pot-au-feu stewing meat, if you are serving it within 2 days of preparing it
* The pot-au-feu vegetables (keeps for 3 days)

Place in the freezer:
* The pot-au-feu stewing meat, if you are serving it more than 2 days after preparing it
* The samosas
* The haddock brandade, in its gratin dish, covered with clingfilm
* The velouté
* The marrowbones with a little broth
* The slices of rustic bread, in an airtight container
* The haddock and coconut milk soup

Place the mixture in a bowl to make the stuffing for the samosas.

16 Place the broken pieces of vegetables in the large mixing bowl to make the velouté. Add 1 potato, the remaining cream, 2 ladles of pot-au-feu broth from the pan and a little salt and pepper. Blend thoroughly using the stick blender. Store in a glass jar.

17 Add the marrowbones to the pan, then continue cooking for as long as time permits (ideally a further 1½ hours).

18 Preheat the oven to 180°C/gas mark 4.
Cut each sheet of filo pastry in half lengthways. Place one sheet of pastry with the long edge facing you. Spoon 1 teaspoon of the samosa stuffing in the left corner of the pastry. Starting at the corner with the filling, fold the pastry diagonally, enclosing the filling to form a triangle. Fold over the pastry again to form a triangle parcel, and keep folding in this way until you reach the end of the pastry strip. Repeat with the remaining pastry and filling. (Although this technique is not complicated, it does take some time to complete. If you need some little hands to help you with this step, kids are always delighted to assist.) Lightly beat 1 egg and brush the samosas with it. Bake for 15 minutes, or until golden and crisp.

Menu #1

Menu #1

Monday

Cooking time:
10 minutes
Preparation time:
10 minutes

Appetizer
Leeks in vinaigrette with devilled eggs

Main
Orzo pasta in beef broth

Ingredients: mustard, vinegar, olive oil, the 8 sections of cooked leeks, remaining uncooked egg, sunflower oil, the 4 hard-boiled eggs, pot-au-feu broth, orzo pasta, salt and pepper
Prepare the vinaigrette. Combine 1 teaspoon (5ml) of mustard with 1 teaspoon of vinegar and a little salt and pepper. Whisk vigorously while drizzling in 2 tablespoons of olive oil a little at a time. Pour the vinaigrette over the leeks. Prepare the filling for the devilled eggs. Combine the 1 raw egg yolk with 1 teaspoon of mustard and a little salt and pepper. Whisk vigorously while adding 4 tablespoons of sunflower oil a little at a time. Peel the hard-boiled eggs. Cut them in half. Remove the yolks, and incorporate them into the mixture. Fill the empty egg white halves with this mixture. Serve with the leeks. Remove and discard the layer of fat from the broth. Cook the pasta in the broth. Serve.
For Tuesday, if you have frozen the pot-au-feu stewing meat, remove it from the freezer and defrost in the refrigerator.

Reheating time:
10 minutes

Tuesday

Pot-au-feu

Ingredients: the pot-au-feu vegetables, pot-au-feu stewing meat, cornichons, mustard, fleur de sel sea salt
Reheat the vegetables and meat. Serve each person one piece of each kind of meat served with the cornichons, mustard and fleur de sel sea salt.
For Wednesday, remove the samosas and the haddock brandade from the freezer and defrost them in the refrigerator.

Reheating time:
10 minutes

Wednesday

Appetizer
Beef and vegetable samosas

Main
Haddock brandade

Ingredients: the samosas, haddock brandade
Preheat the oven to 180°C/gas mark 4, and reheat the samosas and the brandade for 10 minutes. Serve.
For Thursday, remove the velouté, the marrowbones and the bread slices from the freezer and defrost them in the refrigerator.

Thursday

Vegetable velouté, marrow toasts

Reheating time:
15 minutes
Preparation time:
2 minutes

Ingredients: the velouté, marrowbones, slices of bread, fleur de sel sea salt
Reheat the velouté in a saucepan. Reheat the marrowbones with their broth in a small saucepan. Toast the slices of bread. Spread the marrow on the toast, and sprinkle with fleur de sel sea salt.
For Friday, remove the haddock and coconut milk soup from the freezer and defrost it in the refrigerator.

Reheating time:
15 minutes

Friday

Haddock and coconut milk soup

Ingredients: the haddock and coconut milk soup
Reheat the soup in a saucepan, and serve.

Menu #2

Menu #2

Shopping list
Menu #2

Fruit / Vegetables

* 500g button mushrooms
* 2 leeks
* 4 carrots
* ½ red cabbage, about 250g, sell-by date > 3 or 4 days
* 1kg Charlotte (or waxy) potatoes
* 250g lamb's lettuce, sell-by date > 2 days
* 1 small bunch red grapes
* 1 Pink Lady or Golden Delicious apple
* 2 shallots
* 2 onions
* 4 garlic cloves
* 1 small knob of fresh root ginger, grated (optional)

Meat / Fish

* 150g smoked lardons or diced turkey
* 1kg stewing veal
* 16 chicken wings
* 1 chorizo sausage

Refrigerator

* 4 large eggs
* 400ml double cream
* 450g crème fraîche
* about 110g grated Gruyère cheese
* 1 sheet of ready-rolled shortcrust pastry

Basics

* Mustard
* Cornflour
* Dried thyme
* Whole nutmeg
* Wine vinegar
* Olive oil
* Salt, black pepper

Store cupboard

* 500g ready-to-eat lentils
* 250g white rice
* 50g pitted black olives
* 100ml port or red wine
* 1 large can tomato pureé (about 350g)
* Soy sauce
* Honey
* Tomato ketchup

Monday

Quiche Lorraine*

Tuesday

Appetizer
Leek and potato soup

Main
Caramelized chicken wings

Thursday

Cream of lentils, mushrooms and carrots

Friday

Spicy veal stew

Wednesday

Appetizer
Red cabbage, grape and apple salad

Main
Slow-cooked veal and chorizo* stew

*For a pork-free menu, replace the lardons in the quiche with diced turkey meat, and the chorizo with a pinch of chilli powder.

Set up

If you have enough work space, set out all the ingredients needed for this cooking session. This includes everything except the lamb's lettuce, the grapes, apple, lentils and rice. This allows you to have everything at your fingertips and to not lose time searching for the ingredients in the store cupboard or refrigerator.

Set out the necessary equipment:

* ✻ 1 lidded cast-iron casserole or stockpot
* ✻ 1 (20cm) flan tin
* ✻ Ceramic baking beans (or dried beans)
* ✻ 1 small saucepan
* ✻ 1 medium saucepan
* ✻ 1 large mixing bowl
* ✻ 1 frying pan
* ✻ 1 stick blender
* ✻ 1 small grater or zester (for the nutmeg)
* ✻ 5 containers: 3 large + 1 medium + 1 small for the vinaigrette
* ✻ Kitchen paper, baking paper

Everything is now ready for a cooking time of 1¾ hours.

1 Peel and thinly slice the onions and garlic cloves. Cut the veal into cubes. In the cast-iron casserole, heat 1 tablespoon (15ml) of olive oil until warm, then add half the onions and garlic, the veal cubes, 1 teaspoon of salt and a little pepper. Cook for 10 minutes.

2 Meanwhile, peel all of the potatoes and carrots. Cut the potatoes into large dice, and cut the carrots into rounds.

3 To the pan, add ½ teaspoon of thyme and all of the tomato purée. Stir to thoroughly combine. Add the port, then add just enough water to cover the meat. Add three-quarters of the diced potatoes,

one-third of the carrot rounds and the chorizo, cut into thick slices. Simmer, covered, for 1¼ hours.

4 Preheat the oven to 190°C/gas mark 5. Grease the flan tin. Line the tin with the pastry, gently pressing the pastry down into the tin and up the sides. Trim off any excess pastry from around the edges, level with the top of the tin. Prick the bottom of the pastry all over with a fork. Crumple the baking paper included in the pack with the pastry (or use baking paper), place it on top of the pastry in the tin, then fill the tin with the baking beans. Blind bake the pastry case for 25 minutes, or until pale golden.

5 Heat the medium saucepan with 800ml salted water. Cut off the root ends of the leeks and any rough ends of the green portion, then thoroughly wash the leeks (including in between the leaves).

Cut the white portion of the leeks into thick rounds, then dice the green portion. In the saucepan, combine the white portion of the leeks, the remaining potatoes and the remaining onions. Cook for 25 minutes.

6 Fill the small saucepan with salted water and bring it to a boil. Cook the remaining carrot rounds for 20 minutes, or until softened.

7 Prepare the vinaigrette. In the small container, add 2 tablespoons of mustard, ½ teaspoon of salt and 1 pinch of pepper. Add 4 tablespoons of vinegar and stir to combine. Slowly add 8 tablespoons of olive oil while whisking vigorously.

8 Prepare the quiche filling. In the mixing bowl, beat together the eggs with ½ teaspoon of salt, a little pepper and some freshly grated nutmeg. Whisk in the cream.

9 In the frying pan without any added fat, brown the lardons for 5 minutes over high heat. Dab any excess fat from the pan using kitchen paper. Add the cooked lardons to the bottom of the pre-baked pastry case, distribute the Gruyère over the top, and pour in the filling. Bake for 30 minutes, or until golden on top.

10 To the saucepan with the leeks and potatoes, add 2 tablespoons of the crème fraîche, and thoroughly blend using the stick blender.

11 Peel and thinly slice the shallots. In the frying pan, heat 1 tablespoon of olive oil until warm. Add the shallots, the remaining garlic and ½ teaspoon of salt. Cook gently for 5 minutes, then add the diced leek greens. Briefly wash the mushrooms and thinly slice them. Add them to the pan. Cook for 5 minutes.

12 Cut half of the cooked carrot rounds into small dice. Place them in the medium container.

13 Add the remaining crème fraîche to the frying pan, then add 1 tablespoon of cornflour. Cook for 5 minutes, or until slightly thickened. Add one-third of this mixture to the container with the diced carrots; this will serve as the cream for the lentils on Thursday.

It's all done! Leave to cool.

Place in the refrigerator:
* The quiche Lorraine, in its tin (keeps for 2 days)
* The soup, in its pan (keeps for 3 days)
* The chicken wings, in their marinade (keeps for 3 days)
* The vinaigrette (keeps for 1 week)
* The red cabbage (keeps for 1 week)

Place in the freezer:
* The veal and chorizo stew
* The creamed vegetables for the lentils
* The veal stew

<u>14</u> In the frying pan, place the cooked carrot rounds. Remove half the pieces of veal from the casserole and place them in the frying pan. Stir well to combine.

<u>15</u> Add the olives to the casserole, and continue cooking for 10 minutes.

<u>16</u> Prepare the marinade for the chicken wings. In a large container, add 6 tablespoons of soy sauce, 4 tablespoons of honey, 2 tablespoons of tomato ketchup and the grated ginger (if using). Stir to combine, then immerse the chicken wings in the marinade.

<u>17</u> Shred the red cabbage and place it in an airtight container.

Each night's prep

Menu #2

Monday

Quiche Lorraine

Reheating time:
10 minutes

Ingredients: the quiche Lorraine, lamb's lettuce, half the vinaigrette
Reheat the quiche for 10 minutes in the oven preheated to 180°C/gas mark 4. Serve with lamb's lettuce and vinaigrette.

Reheating time:
10 minutes
Cooking time:
10 minutes

Tuesday

Appetizer
Leek and potato soup

Main
Caramelized chicken wings

Ingredients: the marinated chicken wings, the leek and potato soup, black pepper
Preheat the oven to 250°C/gas mark 9. Place the chicken wings with their marinade in a baking dish, and bake for about 10 minutes, just until they are well caramelized. Reheat the soup for 10 minutes over low heat, season with a little pepper and serve.
For Wednesday, remove the veal and chorizo stew from the freezer and defrost it in the refrigerator.

Wednesday

Reheating time:
15 minutes
Preparation time:
10 minutes

Appetizer
Red cabbage, grape and apple salad

Main
Slow-cooked veal and chorizo stew

Ingredients: the thawed veal and chorizo stew, the apple, grapes, red cabbage, remaining vinaigrette
Reheat the stew for 15 minutes over low heat. Slice the apple into thin wedges. Cut the grapes in half and remove any seeds. Add the grated cabbage, apple slices and grapes to a large bowl. Add the vinaigrette, stir to combine, and serve.
For Thursday, remove the container with the creamed vegetables from the freezer and defrost it in the refrigerator.

Thursday

Cream of lentils, mushrooms and carrots

Reheating time:
10 minutes

Ingredients: the lentils, creamed vegetables
Top the lentils with the creamed vegetables. Reheat the dish in either a saucepan or the microwave, according to your preference.
For Friday, remove the veal stew from the freezer and defrost it in the refrigerator.

Reheating time:
15 minutes
Cooking time:
10 minutes

Friday

Spicy veal stew

Ingredients: the rice, veal stew
Cook the rice according to the packet instructions. Reheat the veal stew according to your preferences, in either a saucepan or the microwave. Serve with the rice.

Menu #3

Menu #3

Fruit / Vegetables

* 1 small celeriac
* 1 parsnip
* 1 large head of broccoli
* 3 organic oranges
* 3 blood oranges
* 1kg Charlotte (or waxy) potatoes
* 1 small red kuri squash (onion squash)
* 1 carrot
* 1 handful of bean sprouts
* 1 bunch of parsley
* 1 onion
* 1 (5cm) knob of fresh root ginger
* 1 shallot
* 7 garlic cloves

Meat / Fish

* 4 small duck breasts
* 450g frozen small scallops

Refrigerator

* 4 large eggs
* 800ml double cream
* 225g crème fraîche
* 1 litre low-fat milk
* 1 small fresh goats' cheese (about 60g)

Store cupboard

* 225g dried Chinese wheat noodles
* 425g can chickpeas
* 200g quinoa
* 250g spaghetti
* Honey
* 60g raw or toasted unsalted hazelnuts
* Dried thyme
* Soy sauce
* Quatre épices spice blend
* 100ml white wine

Basics
* Olive oil
* Whole nutmeg
* Cornflour
* Curry powder
* Ground cumin
* Salt, black pepper

Monday

Appetizer
Celeriac and parsnip
soup with scallops

Main
Crustless goats' cheese
and broccoli quiche

Tuesday

Duck breast à l'orange,
scalloped potatoes

Wednesday

Appetizer
Chickpea and orange
salad

Main
Roasted squash, quinoa,
goats' cheese, hazelnuts

Thursday

Duck and noodle
Chinese stir-fry

Friday

Scallop spaghetti

Steps
Menu #3

Set up

If you have enough work space, set out all the ingredients needed for this cooking session. This includes everything except the bean sprouts, duck breasts, scallops, crème fraîche, wheat noodles, chickpeas, spaghetti, cumin, quatre épices spice blend, and white wine. This allows you to have everything at your fingertips and to not lose time searching for the ingredients in the store cupboard or refrigerator.

Set out the necessary equipment:
- ✳ 1 medium saucepan
- ✳ 1 large saucepan
- ✳ 1 mixing bowl
- ✳ 1 food processor or mandoline slicer
- ✳ 1 small grater or zester (for the orange zest and nutmeg)
- ✳ 2 gratin dishes (or shallow baking dishes)
- ✳ 1 sieve
- ✳ 1 (20cm) round cake tin
- ✳ 1 stick blender
- ✳ 1 salad spinner (or clean tea towel)
- ✳ 1 small bowl
- ✳ 8 containers: 1 large + 2 medium + 5 small
- ✳ 2 small lidded glass jars (for the toasted hazelnuts and the garlic and shallots)
- ✳ Kitchen paper

Everything is now ready for a cooking time of 2 hours.

1 Preheat the oven to 160°C/gas mark 3. Peel the potatoes. Very thinly slice them using the food processor or mandoline; do not rinse them. Peel 4 of the garlic cloves, finely chop them, and set them aside in a small bowl.

2 Arrange half the potato slices in a gratin dish. Season with salt, grate a little fresh nutmeg on top, then top with ½ teaspoon of chopped garlic. Arrange the remaining potato slices on top, and season with salt and a little freshly grated nutmeg. Pour 200ml of the cream and 500ml of the milk over the top of the potatoes. Bake on a shelf set near the bottom of the oven for 1½ hours, or until golden on top and bubbling.

3 In the medium saucepan, bring salted water to a boil. Cut the broccoli into florets. Place two-thirds of the florets into the boiling water. Cook for 10 minutes. Set aside the remaining florets in a medium container.

4 Prepare the quiche filling. In the mixing bowl, lightly beat the eggs. Add 400ml of the cream, ½ teaspoon of garlic and 1 tablespoon of cornflour. Season with salt and pepper. Dice half the goats' cheese. Drain the parboiled broccoli florets and distribute them and the diced goats' cheese on the bottom of the cake tin. Pour the quiche filling over the top. Bake for 40 minutes, or until golden, on a shelf placed near the top of the oven.

5 To the large saucepan, add the remaining 500ml of milk and 200ml of water. Season with salt and

bring to a simmer. Peel the celeriac and parsnip. Cut them into large dice. Place them in the saucepan and cook for 20 minutes or until softened.

6 Zest the organic oranges; set the zest aside. Peel the oranges and cut out each segment with a knife, cutting between the white membrane. Press the empty membranes of the oranges over an airtight container to release their juice; reserve. Place the orange segments and zest in the juice.

7 Repeat these steps with the blood oranges (minus the zest), and place the juice and segments in a separate small airtight container.

8 In the medium saucepan, bring salted water to a boil. Thoroughly rinse the quinoa in the sieve. Cook the quinoa for 15 minutes, or just until tender, in the boiling water, then drain.

9 Wash the red kuri squash. Using a large knife, cut the squash in half and peel (reserve the skin; it can be eaten). Scrape out the seeds. Slice the flesh, then dice it. Place the flesh in the second gratin dish with the 3 whole garlic cloves, 1 tablespoon of thyme, 3 tablespoons of olive oil and some salt and pepper. After the potato gratin has finished cooking, increase the oven temperature to 200°C/gas mark 6 and place the baking dish with the squash on a shelf near the top of the oven. Bake for 30 minutes, or until tender when pierced with a fork.

10 Peel the carrot and cut it into julienne (thin matchsticks). Place the strips into a container with the raw broccoli florets.

11 Peel and thinly slice the shallot. Place the slices in a small jar with half the remaining chopped garlic, and seal the jar so that it's airtight.

12 Peel and thinly slice the onion and ginger. Place them in an airtight container with the remaining chopped garlic.

13 In an airtight container, combine 4 tablespoons of soy sauce with 4 tablespoons of honey.

14 Using the stick blender, blend the celeriac and parsnip with the remaining cream and ½ teaspoon of curry powder.

It's all done! Leave to cool.

Place in the refrigerator:
* The cooked quinoa (keeps for 3 to 4 days)
* The soup, in the saucepan (keeps for 3 days)
* The quiche (keeps for 3 days)
* The scalloped potatoes (keeps for 3 days)
* The segments, zest and juice of the organic oranges
* The segments and juice of the blood oranges
* The roasted squash, in its gratin dish (keeps for 4 days)
* The julienned carrots and the remaining broccoli
  (keeps for 1 week)
* The sliced onion with the garlic and ginger (keeps for 1 week)
* The chopped shallot and garlic (keeps for 1 week)
* The honey–soy sauce mixture (keeps for 1 week)
* The parsley (keeps for 1 week)

Store cupboard:
* The chopped toasted hazelnuts

Nothing requires freezing for this menu.

15 Wash the parsley, place in the salad spinner and spin to dry (or gently dry with the tea towel). Place it in a large container between 2 sheets of kitchen paper.

16 If the hazelnuts are not toasted, toast them in the oven for 5 minutes. Roughly chop them and place them in the jar.

Menu #3

Monday

Appetizer
Celeriac and parsnip soup with scallops

Main
Crustless goats' cheese and broccoli quiche

Reheating time:
15 minutes
Cooking time:
1 minute
Preparation time:
1 minute

Ingredients: the celeriac and parsnip soup, olive oil, one-quarter of the scallops (about 115g), curry powder, 4 sprigs of parsley, the crust-free quiche, salt

Preheat the oven to 160°C/gas mark 3. Reheat the quiche for 10 minutes. Meanwhile, reheat the soup in its saucepan over low heat. When the soup is warm, heat 1 tablespoon of olive oil in a small frying pan. Cook the scallops over high heat for 30 seconds on each side. Season lightly with salt and sprinkle them with a pinch of curry powder. Divide the scallops among individual bowls of soup. Top with a little chopped parsley. Serve.

Reheating time:
10 minutes
Cooking time:
10 minutes
Preparation time:
5 minutes

Tuesday

Duck breast à l'orange, scalloped potatoes

Ingredients: the scalloped potatoes, duck breasts, quatre épices spice blend, container with the organic orange segments, zest and juice, half the quantity of the honey-soy sauce mixture

Preheat the oven to 160°C/gas mark 3, and reheat the potatoes for 10 minutes.

Meanwhile, make 4 incisions crossways along each duck breast using the tip of a knife. Heat a large frying pan without any added fat. Place the duck breasts skin side down, and cook over high heat for 7 minutes. Pour out any excess fat from the frying pan, then continue cooking for 3 minutes over medium heat. Add ½ teaspoon of the quatre épices spice blend to the frying pan, then pour in the orange juice to deglaze the pan, and the half quantity of the honey–soy sauce mixture. Boil for 30 seconds, then turn off the heat. Set aside 1 cooked duck breast for Thursday's recipe. Thinly slice the remaining 3 breasts, arrange them in a serving dish, and top them with the orange zest. Pour the sauce (while it's still very warm) over the top, and decorate with the orange segments.

Wednesday

Appetizer
Chickpea and orange salad

Main
Roasted squash, quinoa, goats' cheese, hazelnuts

Ingredients: the chickpeas, segments and juice of the blood oranges, the ground cumin, olive oil, 10 sprigs of parsley, the roasted squash, cooked quinoa, remaining goat's cheese, toasted hazelnuts, salt and pepper

Drain and rinse the chickpeas. Place them in a large bowl. Add the orange juice and segments, ½ teaspoon of cumin, 3 tablespoons of olive oil and salt and pepper. Chop the parsley and add it to the bowl. Stir to combine, and serve.

Preheat the oven to 180°C/gas mark 4, and reheat the squash for 10 minutes. Reheat the quinoa in the microwave and top it with the diced squash and its juice. Dice the goats' cheese, and distribute it and the toasted hazelnuts on top.

Thursday

Duck and noodle Chinese stir-fry

Cooking time:
10 minutes
Preparation time:
5 minutes

Ingredients: the Chinese noodles, olive oil, container with the onion, garlic and ginger, the julienned carrots and the broccoli florets, remaining duck breast, the bean sprouts, remaining honey-soy sauce mixture

Place the noodles in a bowl with 2 litres of very hot water for 4 minutes. Heat 3 tablespoons of olive oil in a sauté pan. Add the sliced onion, garlic, ginger, julienned carrots and broccoli florets. Cook for 4 minutes over high heat, stirring frequently. Very thinly slice the duck breast and remove the fat. Add the breast and bean sprouts to the pan. Cook for 2 minutes. Add the drained noodles and the honey-soy sauce mixture. Stir to combine and serve.

Cooking time:
15 minutes
Preparation time:
5 minutes

Friday

Scallop spaghetti

Ingredients: the spaghetti, olive oil, shallots and garlic, remaining frozen scallops, the white wine, crème fraîche, remaining parsley, salt and pepper

Cook the spaghetti in boiling water. Heat 1 tablespoon of olive oil in a sauté pan until warm. Add the shallots and garlic and ½ teaspoon of salt. Cook for 3 minutes over low heat, then add the scallops, and cook for 1 minute on each side over high heat. Set aside off the heat. Deglaze the pan with the wine, add the crème fraîche, and sprinkle with chopped parsley. Add the spaghetti and reserved scallops. Stir to combine, season with salt and pepper and serve.

Menu #4

Shopping list

Menu #4

Fruit / Vegetables

* 10 carrots
* 2 turnips
* 1 kohlrabi
* 1.5kg waxy potatoes
* 1 pre-cooked beetroot
* 1 curly lettuce
* 1 bunch of parsley
* 6 onions
* 3 garlic cloves

Basics

* 3 bay leaves
* Cornflour
* Mustard
* Wine vinegar
* Olive oil, sunflower oil
* Salt, black pepper

Meat / Fish

* 600g fresh whiting fish fillets
* 800g bacon joint
* 1 smoked sausage
* 4 slices ham
* 150g smoked lardons
* 4 fillet steaks

Refrigerator

* 6 large eggs
* 800ml double cream
* 110g Comté cheese, grated
* 1 wheel Reblochon cheese
* 150g Roquefort (or other blue) cheese

Store cupboard

* 4 brioche buns, 8 thick slices white bread
* 400g green lentils
* 250g white rice
* 1 preserved lemon
* 100ml white wine
* 1 tablespoon drained capers
* 4 cornichons (gherkins)

Monday

Bacon in lentils

Tuesday

Tartiflette and crudités

Wednesday

Appetizer
Stuffed brioche buns

Main
Fishballs with winter vegetables

Thursday

Appetizer
Warm lentil salad, gribiche sauce

Main
Fillet steak, Roquefort sauce

Friday

Croque monsieur

Steps

Menu #14

Set up

If you have enough work space, set out all the ingredients needed for this cooking session. This includes everything except the beetroot, ham, beef fillet stealks, half the cream, 4 eggs, Comté, rice, white sandwich bread, capers, cornichons, and sunflower oil. This allows you to have everything at your fingertips and to not lose time searching for the ingredients in the store cupboard or refrigerator. Set out the necessary equipment:

* 1 lidded cast-iron casserole or small stockpot
* 1 large stockpot (or very large saucepan)
* 1 small saucepan
* 2 large saucepans
* 2 large bowls
* 1 small bowl
* 1 frying pan
* 1 baking dish (for the tartiflette)
* 1 food processor
* 1 salad spinner (or clean tea towel)
* 7 containers: 3 large + 2 medium + 2 small
* Kitchen paper, baking paper, airtight storage bag

Everything is now ready for a cooking time of 2 hours 5 minutes.

1 Thoroughly rinse the bacon joint under cold water to remove excess salt. Soak it for 5 minutes in a large bowl filled with cold water.

2 Peel all of the onions. Set aside 1 whole onion, then finely chop the remaining onions. Set the chopped onions aside in a large bowl.

3 Place the bacon joint in the large stockpot and cover it with cold water. Add the whole onion and 2 bay leaves. Bring to a boil, skim off any fat from the surface and cook for 1½ hours.

4 Meanwhile, place the lardons and 3 tablespoons of the chopped onions in the frying pan without any added fat. Cook for 10 minutes over medium heat.

5 Preheat the oven to 180°C/gas mark 4. Peel and finely chop the garlic cloves. Place them in the small bowl.

6 Prepare the tartiflette. Peel the potatoes and cut them into thin rounds. In the baking dish, arrange half the potato rounds and add ½ teaspoon of the garlic and the onion-lardons mixture. Top with the remaining potato rounds, then pour in about 60ml of the white wine, 300ml of the cream, and season generously with salt and pepper. Cut the Reblochon wheel crossways in half, and place the halves in the centre of the baking dish lying flat. Bake for 50 minutes, or until golden and the cheese has melted.

7 In the cast-iron casserole, heat 2 tablespoons of olive oil until warm. Add the remaining onions, half the garlic and 1 teaspoon of salt. Cook for 10 minutes over low heat.

8 Peel the carrots. Cut 8 of the carrots into rounds, and 2 into julienne (thin matchstick strips).

9 Pour the remaining wine into the casserole, and cook until the wine has evaporated. Add the carrot rounds and 250ml water.

10 Peel the turnips and kohlrabi. Cut into cubes, apart from half the kohlrabi that you will cut into julienne. Add the cubed vegetables to the pan in a single layer, and cook for 20 minutes without stirring. Place the julienned kohlrabi in an airtight container with the julienned carrots.

Menu #4

11 Add the smoked sausage to the pan containing the bacon joint.

12 In a large saucepan, bring water (not salted) to a boil. Rinse the lentils. Cook them for 20 minutes in the boiling water with 1 bay leaf.

13 Slice off the top of each brioche bun, then pull out the interior crumb (creating a bread bowl); set aside. Seal the hollow brioche shells inside the airtight storage bag, and set them in the refrigerator.

14 Wash the parsley and gently dry it in the salad spinner (or with a clean tea towel). Repeat these same steps with the lettuce. Place the parsley and lettuce in separate airtight containers between 2 sheets of kitchen paper.

15 Prepare the whiting fishballs. Remove the bones from the fish fillets. In the food processor, place the reserved brioche crumb, the fish, the pulp from half the preserved lemon, ½ teaspoon of garlic, 2 sprigs of parsley and some salt and pepper. Pulse to combine, just until the mixture comes together. Shape the mixture into balls using the palms of your hands.

16 Remove the turnip and kohlrabi cubes and several carrot rounds from the casserole, and place them in a large saucepan. Add a ladle of the cooking juices and half the remaining preserved lemon. Place the fishballs on top, cover, and cook for 10 minutes.

It's all done! Leave to cool.

Place in the refrigerator:
* The bacon in lentils, in its pan (keeps for 2 days)
* The tartiflette (keeps for 3 days)
* The brioche buns in the airtight storage bag (keeps for 4 days)
* The cooked lentils (keeps for 5 days)
* The hard-boiled eggs (keeps for 5 days)
* The rinsed lettuce (keeps for 1 week)
* The vegetable sticks (keeps for 1 week)
* The washed parsley (keeps for 1 week)
* The vinaigrette (keeps for 1 week)

Place in the freezer:
* The fillet steaks, if you have purchased them from a butcher or if their sell-by date is less than 5 days
* The Roquefort sauce
* The fishballs with the winter vegetables

17 Drain the lentils. Add half the lentils to the pan with the carrots. Add the bacon joint and the cooked sausage (cut into pieces) to the pan with 1 ladle of the cooking juices. Cook for 10 minutes. Set aside the remaining cooked lentils in a medium container.

18 Prepare the Roquefort sauce. In the small saucepan, heat the Roquefort (diced) over low heat. Add 100ml of the cream and the remaining garlic. Bring to a boil, then lower the heat. Add 1 tablespoon of cornflour, and season generously with salt and pepper. Transfer the sauce to an airtight container. Wash the saucepan.

19 Fill the small saucepan with water and bring it to a boil. Add 2 eggs and cook them for 10 minutes.

20 Prepare the vinaigrette. Combine 2 tablespoons of mustard, 3 tablespoons of vinegar, 1 teaspoon of salt, and a little pepper. Whisk vigorously while adding 6 tablespoons of olive oil a little at a time.

Menu #4

Each night's prep

Menu #4

Monday

Bacon in lentils

<u>Reheating time:</u>
15 minutes

Ingredients: the bacon in lentils, 4 sprigs of parsley
Reheat the bacon in lentils for 15 minutes. Just before serving, chop the parsley and sprinkle it over the bacon.

<u>Reheating time:</u>
10 minutes
<u>Preparation time:</u>
2 minutes

Tuesday

Tartiflette and crudités

Ingredients: the tartiflette, half the washed lettuce, the vegetable sticks, half the vinaigrette
Preheat the oven to 180°C/gas mark 4, and reheat the tartiflette for 10 minutes.
In a large bowl, serve the lettuce with the vegetable sticks and the vinaigrette.
<u>For Wednesday, remove the fishballs from the freezer and defrost them in the refrigerator.</u>

Wednesday

Appetizer
Stuffed brioche buns

Main
Fishballs with winter vegetables

<u>Reheating time:</u>
15 minutes
<u>Cooking time:</u>
10 minutes
<u>Preparation time:</u>
10 minutes

Ingredients: the remaining 4 eggs, the hollow brioche buns, 200ml of the cream, one-third of the Comté, 4 parsley sprigs, 4 lettuce leaves, the vinaigrette, rice, defrosted meatballs, salt and pepper
Preheat the oven to 220°C/gas mark 7. Break 1 egg into each hollow brioche, add 1 teaspoon of cream, top with a sprinkling of Comté, season with salt and pepper, and sprinkle a little parsley on top. Set the buns in a baking dish, and bake for 10 minutes. Serve with a small salad and some vinaigrette (reserving some of the vinaigrette for Friday). Cook the rice according to the packet instructions. Reheat the fishballs in a saucepan for 10 minutes. Add the remaining cream, then continue reheating for 5 more minutes. Serve with the rice.
<u>For Thursday, remove the Roquefort sauce from the freezer and the fillet steaks, if you have frozen them, and defrost in the refrigerator.</u>

Reheating time:
10 minutes
Cooking time:
8 minutes
Preparation time:
10 minutes

Thursday

Appetizer
Warm lentil salad, gribiche sauce

Main
Beef tenderloin, Roquefort sauce

Ingredients: the cooked lentils, cornichons, half the remaining parsley, the hard-boiled eggs, 2 tablespoons mustard, 3 tablespoons sunflower oil, 1 tablespoon wine vinegar, the capers, defrosted Roquefort sauce, fillet steaks, salt and pepper

Gently reheat the lentils in the microwave. Finely chop the cornichons and parsley. Peel the hard-boiled eggs, cut them in half, and remove the yolks. Cut the whites into small dice. Make a gribiche sauce. Crumble the yolks into a large bowl and add the mustard and some salt and pepper; stir to combine. Slowly drizzle in the sunflower oil while whisking to combine. Stir in the vinegar, capers, diced egg whites and the chopped cornichons and parsley. Serve the warm lentils combined with the gribiche sauce.

In a small saucepan, reheat the Roquefort cheese sauce for 10 minutes over low heat. In a frying pan, cook the fillet steaks for about 4 minutes on each side, more or less according to your preference. Season with salt and pepper and serve with the sauce.

Friday

Cooking time:
10 minutes
Preparation time:
10 minutes

Croque monsieur

Ingredients: the remaining double cream, remaining grated Comté, the 8 slices of sandwich bread, ham, cooked beetroot, remaining lettuce, vinaigrette, parsley, salt and pepper

Preheat the oven to 220°C/gas mark 7. In a bowl, combine the cream with half the remaining Comté, ½ teaspoon of salt and a little pepper. On top of 1 slice of bread, place a folded piece of ham, sprinkle with 1 handful of grated Comté, and top with a second slice of bread. Spread 1 tablespoon of the Comté-cream mixture on top, and place the sandwich on a baking-paper-lined baking sheet. Repeat these steps with the remaining bread slices. Bake the croque monsieur for 10 minutes. Cut the beetroot into rounds, and serve on top of the lettuce with the vinaigrette and a sprinkle of chopped parsley.

Spring menu

Spring menu #1

Monday

Garlic leg of lamb, roasted vegetables, cannellini beans

Tuesday

Starter: Asparagus soup
Main: Herb-crusted fresh cod

Wednesday

Shepherd's pie

Thursday

Starter: White-bean hummus, vegetable sticks
Main: Pasta with asparagus and fresh cod

Friday

Minestrone

Spring menu #2

Monday

Salmon and watercress pie

Tuesday

Starter: Radish toasts
Main: Tarragon chicken

Wednesday

Lentil dhal

Thursday

Starter: Creamy radish-leaf spread
Main: Caesar salad

Friday

Green curry monkfish

Spring menu #3

Monday

Starter: Fennel marinated in olive oil and lemon
Main: Turkey cordon bleu*

Tuesday

Marinated skirt steak, puréed baby carrots

Wednesday

Spinach and ricotta stuffed shells

Thursday

Salad Niçoise

Friday

Starter: Warm goats' cheese toasts
Main: Prawn pad thai

Spring menu #4

Monday

Pot-roast with spring vegetables

Tuesday

Starter: Cauliflower in caper vinaigrette
Main: Savoury cheesecake

Wednesday

Starter: Smoked mackerel rillettes
Main: Chicken puttanesca

Thursday

Spiced bulgur with cauliflower, broccoli and chickpeas

Friday

Smoked mackerel tagliatelle and vegetables

*For a pork-free menu, replace the ham with turkey breast

Summer menus

Summer menu #1

Monday

Starter: Quinoa tabbouleh
Main: Chicken legs and ratatouille

Tuesday

Prosciutto and vegetable pizza*

Wednesday

Courgette, olive and chicken pasta

Thursday

Starter: Goats' cheese and ratatouille turnovers
Main: Stuffed tomatoes and rice

Friday

Family-size vegetable pasta salad

Summer menu #2

Monday

Family-size potato, salmon, mixed leaf, onion and cucumber salad

Tuesday

Starter: Greek lentil salad
Main: Stuffed courgettes

Wednesday

Moussaka

Thursday

Fish stew with dill + rice

Friday

Starter: Pea, feta and mint soup
Main: Lentil balls in tomato sauce with green beans

*For a pork-free menu, replace the prosciutto with turkey breast

Summer menu #3

Monday

Marinated chicken kebabs with wheat and roasted vegetables

Tuesday

Merguez sausage with couscous

Wednesday

Starter: Aubergine caviar
Main: Spanish omelette

Thursday

Summer bruschetta

Friday

Starter: Bell peppers marinated in garlic and olive oil
Main: Tunisian spaghetti

Summer menu #4

Monday

Starter: Courgette gazpacho
Main: Tuna and tomato quiche

Tuesday

Prawn and pineapple fried rice

Wednesday

Starter: Tzatziki sauce
Main: Courgette and ham loaf*

Thursday

Chickpea burgers

Friday

Farfalle and smoked salmon salad

*For a pork-free menu, replace the ham with turkey breast

Autumn menus

Autumn menu #1

Monday

Pasta with beef cheek sauce

Tuesday

Starter: **Hummus with crudités**
Main: **Butternut-chestnut soup with lardons** (or smoked tofu)

Wednesday

Starter: **Lamb's lettuce, green apple and cashew salad**
Main: **Shepherd's pie**

Thursday

Butternut squash and spinach fried rice, toasted cashews

Friday

Vietnamese pho

Autumn menu #2

Monday

Starter: **Cauliflower velouté with sautéed prawns**
Main: **Polenta pizza with mushrooms**

Tuesday

Sweet potato* and chicken curry

Wednesday

Cauliflower and potato gratin with ham**

Thursday

Starter: **Cabbage, egg and cherry tomato salad with creamy dressing**
Main: **Linguine*** with garlic cream, rocket, walnuts and Parmesan**

Friday

Cod and sweet potato* fish pie

*If you do not like sweet potatoes, replace half the quantity with carrots (for the curry) and the other half with potatoes (for the fish pie), following the instructions exactly as written.
**For a pork-free menu, replace the ham with turkey breast
***For a gluten-free menu, use gluten-free pasta

Autumn menu #3

Monday

Starter: Tuna rillettes chicory bites
Main: Turnip, honey and goats' cheese tart Tatin

Tuesday

Lamb tagine with quince

Wednesday

Starter: Spinach velouté
Main: Potato, leek, onion and bacon gratin*

Thursday

Lamb koftas, pan-fried carrots, turnips and chickpeas with cumin

Friday
Salmon and spinach lasagne

*For a pork-free menu, replace the lardons with smoked tofu

Autumn menu #4

Monday

Starter: Cherry tomatoes, Parmesan, pumpkin seeds and thyme in flaky pastry
Main: Vegetarian chilli

Tuesday

Pumpkin and chicken couscous

Wednesday

Ham* and broccoli pasta bake

Thursday

Chicken and vegetable crumble

Friday

Starter: Curried pumpkin soup
Main: Pollack in a shallot sauce with steamed potatoes

*For a pork-free menu, replace the ham with turkey

Winter menus

Winter menu #1

Monday

Starter: **Leeks in vinaigrette with devilled eggs**
Main: **Orzo pasta in beef broth**

Tuesday

Pot-au-feu

Wednesday

Starter: **Beef and vegetable samosas**
Main: **Haddock brandade**

Thursday

Vegetable velouté, marrow toasts

Friday

Haddock and coconut milk soup

Winter menu #2

Monday

Quiche Lorraine*

Tuesday

Starter: **Leek and potato soup**
Main: **Caramelized chicken wings**

Wednesday

Starter: **Red cabbage, grape and apple salad**
Main: **Slow-cooked veal and chorizo* stew**

Thursday

Cream of lentils, mushrooms and carrots

Friday

Spicy veal stew

*For a pork-free menu, replace the lardons in the quiche with diced turkey meat and the chorizo with a pinch of chile pepper.

Winter menu #3

Monday

Starter: Celeriac and parsnip soup with scallops
Main: Crustless goats' cheese and broccoli quiche

Tuesday

Duck breast à l'orange, scalloped potatoes

Wednesday

Starter: Chickpea and orange salad
Main: Roasted squash, quinoa, goats' cheese, hazelnuts

Thursday

Duck and noodle Chinese stir-fry

Friday

Scallop spaghetti

Winter menu #4

Monday

Bacon in lentils

Tuesday

Tartiflette and crudités

Wednesday

Starter: Stuffed brioche buns
Main: Fishballs with winter vegetables

Thursday

Starter: Warm lentil salad, gribiche sauce
Main: Fillet steak, Roquefort sauce

Friday

Croque monsieur

Acknowledgements

Thanks to Marin Postel, my editor, for her kindness, availability and professionalism.

Thanks to Céline Le Lamer, Editorial Manager, for her trust and intelligence.

Thanks to Charly Deslandes, my photographer, for his perfect photos, his positive outlook and his incredible efficiency.

Thanks to the Le Creuset brand for the casserole dishes of exceptional quality, which I recommend to everyone; the investment is well worth it. Equal thanks to the brand Greenpan for the ceramic cookware used in this book: frying pans, sauté pans, woks, etc. To try them is to want to use them every day!

Thanks to my local markets and supermarkets for their fresh products: fresh grocer Ben Saïd, fishmonger Forestier, Butcher Stéphane, Charcuterie Le Bon, Miele Primeur (Sandra), Roufia, and the team from my local "La Vie Claire" store.

Thanks to my family for their support: my mum (aka Mami Mumu), Benoit, Alexandre, Fred and Eliott.

And thanks to all my friends who served as testers for the recipes in this book: Caroline, Sakho, JB, Delphine, Florence and Audrey.

Caroline Pessin

An Hachette UK Company
www.hachette.co.uk

First published in France in 2018 as *En 2H Je Cuisine Pour Toute la Semaine* by Hachette Livre

First published in Great Britain in 2019 by Hamlyn,
an imprint of Octopus Publishing Group Ltd
Carmelite House
50 Victoria Embankment
London EC4Y 0DZ
www.octopusbooks.co.uk

All photography by Charly Deslandes

Copyright © 2018 Hachette Livre (Hachette Pratique)

ISBN 978 0 60063 619 9
A CIP catalogue record for this book is available from the British Library.

Printed in Spain
1 3 5 7 9 10 8 6 4 2